Praise for *Hallelujah: Cultivating Advent Traditions with Handel's Messiah*

"Advent is a season of preparation and anticipation. This delightful volume provides meaningful, beautiful, and practical ways to prepare our hearts for the great mystery of Christ's Nativity."
Angelina Stanford • House of Humane Letters

"Waiting has never been so beautiful...Filled with words of wisdom, recipes, and Rollins family memories, *Hallelujah* helps moms rightly focus the season of Advent on waiting for the birth of the King. Simple listening guides make accomplishing each day's reflection doable even in the busiest household, while longer reflections feed a mama's heart. This guide is a treasure you will return to year after year."
Pam Barnhill • "Your Morning Basket Podcast" Host

CINDY ROLLINS

HALLELUJAH

Cultivating Advent Traditions With
Handel's Messiah

Contents

*Cultivating Advent Traditions
with Handel's* Messiah

What is Advent?

I love Christmas! It was inevitable. I was born on St. Nicholas's Day, December 6—a day that falls just when everyone is itching to celebrate, before the fatigue, or even the hint of it, has set into the season. My mother loved the holiday season and celebrated it with vigor in our home. She especially loved giving presents. Unfortunately, she is not a patient person. The minute she bought a present she wanted us to open it. I spent my childhood begging my mom to hide my presents and wait until Christmas. I have always loved the wait. It came as quite a surprise to me when I grew up and found out that what I had called the Christmas season was really a season of celebrating "the wait," the expectation of the coming of Christ. Advent is a whole season of waiting followed by the joy of the consummation of Christmas. The idea of Advent was my first introduction to the idea of a church calendar, and it has taken me years and years to begin to appreciate the meaning of it all. Advent is the first event in the liturgical year. It begins four Sundays before Christmas and typically ends on Christmas Eve.

While it is historically a time of fasting in preparation for the Christmas Eve festivities and the Twelve Days of Christmas that follow, in our family it took on a more American twist.

We always started our holiday celebrations the day after Thanksgiving by bringing out all the Christmas music and Christmas books. We set aside our usual Morning Time[1] routine in order to have time to read Christmas books and sing Christmas carols. I often interchange the words *Advent* and *Christmas*, understandably so in our culture that begins celebrating Christmas sometime in the middle of Halloween night. Therefore, our family's Advent was always part contemplation and expectation, and part wild celebration. Truthfully, by the time Christmas Day came around we limped into New Year's Eve. The Twelve Days of Christmas that began with Christmas Day were for the most part unknown and uncelebrated as we longed, after a month of feasting and fun, to return to normalcy. I say all that because this little book reflects our family's somewhat synchronistic practices. Other families, especially in recent years, as Christians have sought out historical forms, have successfully moved their traditions to be more in line with the church calendar. I think that is a wonderful thing. Hopefully, the ideas in this little volume will be helpful to both strict Advent observers (we won't call them Adventists!) and those who muddy the waters with Christmas celebrations.

> Our family's Advent was always part contemplation and expectation, part wild celebration.

Let the wild ruckus begin!

---

1   Morning Time refers to my homeschooling practice of daily gathering together with my children for a read-aloud time that includes key elements such as Scripture, poetry, hymns, selections from Plutarch's Lives and Shakespeare, and other literature. You can learn more about Morning Time in my book *Handbook for Morning Time*.

Why Messiah?

I n that far-off time before computers or the internet, our family loved Christmas music. We loved it more than most other families I knew. We had a huge collection of Christmas tapes which eventually we converted to Christmas CDs. We had LPs from my childhood, *Christmas with Gisele* comes to mind with the enduring "He's Too Fat for the Chimney," and a series of contemporary Christian Christmas offerings, some of which have actually stood the test of time. Eventually, we even rebought our favorites on iTunes and our family iTunes Holiday playlist is over twenty-four hours long—most of which can now be found on Spotify for free if you don't count those annoying ads. Amidst all that wonderful music is Handel's *Messiah*. There was hardly time to listen to it. I didn't want it to get lost among the shuffle of great Christmas music.

One day while reading through the notes, I realized that the libretto aligned closely to many of the Advent devotionals I used during the month of December. Most of my Advent resources concentrated on prophecies of Christ from the Old Testament, which is exactly what *Messiah* does. Yet *Messiah* goes even further and continues through the birth of Christ, "Hallelujah, the Lord

God Omnipotent reigneth," to the final, more sobering triumph of "Worthy is the Lamb." After noticing this, I decided to structure our December Morning Time around the *Messiah*. I divided the libretto and tracks up into days. For our Advent devotions we read the Bible verses from the Bible, discussed the tracks we would listen to, and then closed our eyes and listened. It was truly perfection—an Advent family devotion that was not too long and could be easily caught up on missed days. No more trying to read pages and pages and pages of missed Advent readings.

> It was truly perfection—an Advent family devotion that was not too long and could be easily caught up on missed days.

Messiah breaks down easily into sections. Most sections include first a recitative, followed by an air or solo, followed by a chorus. These are of varying lengths, from Day 1 which is eleven minutes, to Day 17 which is only a one-minute tenor aria. This book can be read as simply as this: pick up the Bible or read the passages for the day as printed for you. Listen to the tracks given for that day in the listening schedule. *Messiah* movement numbers in this guide correspond to the movement numbers listed on album or Spotify tracks. It isn't even important which recording you use. Families have used all sorts of different recordings of *Messiah* with this devotional.

Our family has done this year after year after year so that *Messiah* is part of our hearts and minds. In addition to this simple method, I sometimes have the whole oratorio playing in the background just as a remembrance.

How to Use This Guide

I have tried to keep this book very simple. Let me tell you a secret. You can use this book any old way you please. You can follow all my suggestions and ideas or you can simply follow the outline of *Messiah* each day. I highly recommend that you do not complicate it too much. Did you have a great St. Nicholas's Day feast last year but feel overwhelmed and tired this year? Guess what? It is okay to skip it or to celebrate it with take-out Chinese. Some years you might make the best molded cookies and some years the cookies crumble to pieces. I have found that crumbled cookies still taste good. Advent is a time of anticipation and joy. What I love most about using *Messiah* as an outline for the season is that it is just so simple.

The "Hallelujah" chorus has been covered by many artists. I won't know if you choose Elvis. I have chosen to use the libretto from the first London performance of *Messiah* in 1743. This was not the first performance of *Messiah*: that happened in Dublin in 1742. My own favorite recording is the Nevill Marriner Academy and Chorus of St. Martin-in-the-Fields. On my recent trip to London, one of the surprises was getting to hear a concert at St. Martin-in-the-Fields. I must say it made me tremble to think of the significance of it, however the modern updates to the church were a bit disturbing. So terribly, terribly modern. I had always imagined a place more, well, medieval, and sitting in a field, perhaps. Nevertheless, it was still quite emotional for me to be in a place so central to my own mothering memories through the much-loved recording of *Messiah*.

I have divided up this book by weeks. Each week contains ideas for things to cook, memorize, and enjoy. Feast days are noted. It is probably ambitious to think you can memorize the Bible passages and poems in one week. Let us return to the imagery of the long haul and save some for next year. No need to stress everyone out by trying to memorize it all.

> I have divided up this book by weeks. Each week contains ideas for things to cook, memorize, and enjoy. Feast days are noted.

I invited several talented friends to contribute to this volume. Greg Wilbur shares background information about Handel's *Messiah* to enrich your listening experience. Each week includes Greg's suggestions before the *Messiah* listening schedule. I'm also thankful for my friends Kerry Williamson, Lynn Bruce, Caitlin Bruce Beauchamp, and Kelly Cumbee for sharing with us stories of their unique Advent traditions. Remember their stories should inspire you to create your own organic traditions, not fill you with panic and frustration. Finally, I asked Thomas Banks, a published poet, essayist and regular on the *Literary Life Podcast* with Angelina Stanford and me, to share with us the history of the Christian church calendar and the early beginnings of Advent observances. I was delighted with his approach and am excited for you to read his essay and poem.

You can use the weekly selection for your Advent Wreath activities. On Sunday light the candle or candles for the week. You can also relight the weekly candles while you are listening to the *Messiah* selections each day. Just buy extra candles in case they burn down. Candles are for burning and they are inexpensive. They are the perfect embodiment of the season so burn, baby, burn.

The Christian Calendar

Thomas Banks

When as students we began the study of a foreign language, one of the first things we committed to memory was that language's names for the days of the week and the months of the year. To learn a language means learning something of the people who speak it as their native tongue, and knowing them means knowing how they set about ordering that part of the world in which they live. A calendar is one of the most natural instruments of order. There has never existed any great civilization that was without its particular means of keeping track of time and seasons. The making of calendars has throughout history been closely interwoven with the religious life of societies, and it is probable that the first calendar-artist was a priest of one sect or another. Our self-understanding as beings subject to time would seem to be inseparable from our accompanying sense of ourselves as beings subject to the gods. The ancient calendar of the Romans took as its Year One what in our Gregorian reckoning is 753 B.C., the year of their city's supposed founding under the rule of Romulus, the son of the god of war. A similar inspiration may be seen in the old Japanese imperial calendar, whose base year was 660 B.C., when the legendary Emperor Jimmu, likewise said to be of divine ancestry, established the foundations of that famous island nation. Every good tale of beginnings needs a god at the back of it.

The origins of the Christian liturgical calendar are nearly as old as the Christian Church. As the Gospel of Christ struck root and grew in the ground of the Roman empire, Christians themselves grew increasingly conscious of the fact that the new faith was a thing distinct from the confession and practice of the venerable Jewish religion from which it had sprung. The principal days of worship within the two confessions were different, as were their respective days of fast and feast. Central to the Gospel narrative was the account of Christ's Passion, which within the first generations of the early Church came to enjoy a position as the "feast of feasts and solemnity of solemnities" in *The Divine Liturgy*. This primacy, as if by natural right, fell to the memorial of Our Lord's Resurrection, and the holy drama of suffering and degradation in the days preceding His triumph once and for all over the empire of death and Hell. This feast was the root from which a thousand others were to spring. Of such importance was it that the proper dating of Pascha, or Easter, was from the first a source of much dispute between one body of Christians and another. We find the question debated in Rome in the second century and England in the seventh. Neither has this point of contention been entirely resolved in our own day.

> The first observances of Christmas did not begin much later in time than those of Easter.

The first observances of Christmas did not begin much later in time than those of Easter. Though the familiar traditions of the Lord's Nativity are relatively new, the fact of the divine birth in the mind of the Church was never a matter of small significance. To every Christian, Christmas perhaps should be more surprising than we often allow it to be; that God or the gods had, in some far distant time, created the world and the first men was a belief shared by most ancients, pagans, Jews, and Christians alike. That God should remake it was quite a new thing, and that He should remake it by becoming a part of what He had made, by taking on the nature of His finest and fallen creation man, sharing man's birth that He might be the source of a new birth, was to most of the thinking world blasphemy or foolishness. Christmas is the commemoration of that foolishness, whose deeper wisdom the shepherds knew when they came to kneel before the infant Christ in the dark time of the closing year. As for the date of Christmas, the early Christian writer St. Hippolytus of Rome mentions the birth of the Savior as having taken place on December 25th ("eight days before the kalends of January") in his *Commentary on the Book of Daniel*, though that date was not yet universally recognized as holding that honor. But no real substitute is to be found among the Church's other primitive documents, and the skepticism that likes to cloud the honest revelry of the December holiday with questions about "when the historic Christ was really born" must be left to the overeducated to argue among themselves.

The birth, death, and resurrection of the Lord were the great luminaries in the constellation of the Christian year, and beside these appeared the lesser lights of the martyrs. Through their witness and sacrifices the Church had grown so quickly that historians have been left at a loss to account for it, and the Church has repaid them ever since with the yearly commemoration of their lives and deaths. Most of these festivals began humbly enough, being held by the friends and loved ones of the martyred believer, often in the place and on the anniversary of his execution. Events of this kind became known in many places as the *dies natalis*, or birthday of the saint, the remembrance of the day such a one was born into a new life and welcomed into a new world above this one. So it is that one service of the Church's calendar is to strengthen her ties of fellowship with the communion of the saints in glory, reminding the Christian on earth of his brothers and sisters in Heaven, where sin and death have no place, and time itself is no more.

> The birth, death, and resurrection of the Lord were the great luminaries in the constellation of the Christian year.

Week 1:
Remembering Prophecy

Remembering Prophecy

The entire Advent season is one of remembrance. We are remembering the birth of Christ, but we are also remembering that his birth was foretold over and over again in the Old Testament. The first half of the *Messiah* rehearses these prophesies. This week we will remember the prophesies from Isaiah, Haggai, Malachi, and Zechariah. I like to have my house all ready to worship and celebrate for the next four weeks, so I get my Christmas tree up—a live one no less—as soon as I can after Thanksgiving. I love to have those four or five weeks of morning devotions with the lights twinkling. We put as many lights on our tree as we can and then we light up plenty of other spaces too. Of course, besides the twinkle lights, we have candles everywhere. Once all the books, music, trees, and decorations are up, then we can truly let the magic happen.

Advent Hymn

O Come, O Come, Emmanuel in English and Latin

This is probably the single most recommended Advent hymn and not without reason. It is beautiful. It is easily sung in both Latin and English, and it reminds us that Advent is not quite a wild celebration but an almost mournful longing. I recommend that you sing this one every morning this week. We liked to let the kids take turns picking Christmas carols each morning after we sang our weekly carol. It has always been important to me that we sing and sing and sing over the season as some of the best Christian music is centered on the themes of Advent and Christmas. I hate missing church during Advent, and I adore that my church fully appreciates the music of Christmas—singing these seasonal hymns from the week after Thanksgiving through Epiphany.

O Come, O Come, Emmanuel

TRANSLATED BY JOHN NEALE, 1818-66
STANZAS 7-8 HENRY SLOANE COFFIN, 1877-1954

O come, O come, Emmanuel,
And ransom captive Israel,
That mourns in lonely exile here
Until the Son of God appear.
Rejoice! Rejoice! Emmanuel
Shall come to thee, O Israel!

O come, Thou Rod of Jesse, free
Thine own from Satan's tyranny;
From depths of hell Thy people save,
And give them in victory o'er the grave.
Rejoice! Rejoice! Emmanuel
Shall come to thee, O Israel!

O come, Thou Dayspring, come and cheer,
Our spirits by Thine advent here,
Disperse the gloomy clouds of night,
And death's dark shadows put to flight.
Rejoice! Rejoice! Emmanuel
Shall come to thee, O Israel!

O come, Thou Key of David, come,
And open wide our heavenly home;
Make safe the way that leads on high,
And close the path to misery.
Rejoice! Rejoice! Emmanuel
Shall come to thee, O Israel!

O come, O come, Thou Lord of might,
Who once from Sinai's flaming height,
In ancient times didst give the law,
In cloud, and majesty, and awe.
Rejoice! Rejoice! Emmanuel
Shall come to thee, O Israel!

O come, Thou Wisdom from on high,
And order all things far and nigh;
To us the path of knowledge show,
and cause us in her ways to go.
Rejoice! Rejoice! Emmanuel
Shall come to thee, O Israel!

O come, Desire of nations,
bind all peoples in one heart and mind;
bid envy, strife and quarrels cease;
fill the whole world with heaven's peace.
Rejoice! Rejoice! Emmanuel
Shall come to thee, O Israel!

O Come, O Come, Emmanuel in Latin

Sometimes it is fun to sing in Latin even if you haven't been studying Latin.

Veni, Veni, Emmanuel

Veni, veni Emmanuel;
captivum solve Israel,
qui gemit in exilio,
privatus dei filio.

Gaude! Gaude! Emmanuel
nascetur pro te, Israel!

Veni, veni, O Oriens;
solare nos adveniens.
Noctis depelle nebulas;
dirasque mortis tenebras.

Gaude! Gaude! Emmanuel
nascetur pro te, Israel!

Veni, clavis Davidica!
Regna reclude cealica;
fac iter tutum superum,
et claude vias inferum.

Gaude! Gaude! Emmanuel
nascetur pro te, Israel!

Advent Scripture Memory

Elizabeth's Song

Luke 1:39-45 (NASB)

39 Now at this time Mary arose and went in a hurry to the hill country, to a city of Judah,

40 and entered the house of Zacharias and greeted Elizabeth.

41 When Elizabeth heard Mary's greeting, the baby leaped in her womb; and Elizabeth was filled with the Holy Spirit.

42 And she cried out with a loud voice and said, "Blessed are you among women, and blessed is the fruit of your womb!

43 "And how has it happened to me, that the mother of my Lord would come to me?

44 "For behold, when the sound of your greeting reached my ears, the baby leaped in my womb for joy.

45 "And blessed is she who believed that there would be a fulfillment of what had been spoken to her by the Lord."

Advent Poetry

Many Christmas poems, such as this one, have been turned into carols. Still, sometimes it is nice to recite the poems without music. Here is my favorite Christmas poem.

In the Bleak Midwinter

CHRISTINA GEORGINA ROSSETTI

In the bleak midwinter, frosty wind made moan,
Earth stood hard as iron, water like a stone;
Snow had fallen, snow on snow, snow on snow,
In the bleak midwinter, long ago.

Our God, Heaven cannot hold Him, nor earth sustain;
Heaven and earth shall flee away when He comes to reign.
In the bleak midwinter a stable place sufficed
The Lord God Almighty, Jesus Christ.

Enough for Him, whom cherubim, worship night and day,
Breastful of milk, and a mangerful of hay;
Enough for Him, whom angels fall before,
The ox and ass and camel which adore.

Angels and archangels may have gathered there,
Cherubim and seraphim thronged the air;
But His mother only, in her maiden bliss,
Worshipped the beloved with a kiss.

What can I give Him, poor as I am?
If I were a shepherd, I would bring a lamb;
If I were a Wise Man, I would do my part;
Yet what I can I give Him: give my heart.

Advent Feast Day

The Feast of St. Nicholas - December 6

For those conflicted about Santa Claus, here is the perfect compromise—celebrate the real St. Nicholas, the holy bishop of Myra. Myra is located in present-day Turkey. You might even want to mix up the reading of stories of Santa Claus with real stories of St. Nicholas. Try "'Twas the Night Before Christmas" ("A Visit from St. Nicholas," by Clement Clarke Moore) or my favorite Santa Claus book, *Jolly Old Santa Claus*, with those lovely George Hinke illustrations, which are almost the perfect mutation of St. Nicholas into Santa Claus. Of course, there are many websites dedicated to the real St. Nicholas and also a few beautiful children's books, too.

St. Nicholas's feast day is traditionally celebrated with molded cookies. A couple years ago I bought a beautiful old-fashioned St. Nicholas mold. I found my own shortbread recipe worked pretty well in the mold, and you cannot beat a good old butter cookie for flavor. You can also find recipes and ideas for cookie molds online. Our "Scotch Shortbread" recipe is on page 121.

Just for Fun

Our family liked to pick "Angels" early in the season. The word *angel* makes no sense here, but we drew names from a hat and each person was then supposed to "bless" the person whose name they drew for the holiday season, ending with buying them a gift to open on Christmas Eve. In fact, in our house it immediately became a logic game to see who could figure out who had whom as quickly as possible. I am not entirely sure how successful the Angels were at blessing their siblings throughout the holiday, but it was fun to get that gift from a sibling on Christmas Eve.

One year, Tim and I left the Angel gift buying—which we ultimately funded until the kids got older—a little too late. We took all the kids to Walmart, tried to divide ourselves up so that no one was with the person buying their gift and bought all the Angel gifts while trying not to run into each other in the toy section. Here goeth madness. Some years when things were especially lean, the only gifts the kids got were from their relatives and their Angels. One happy memory I have is that my children always did seem to appreciate their gifts no matter how lean the Christmas. But not every year was lean. One year we counted over fifty balls of various sorts and sports wrapped under the tree next to those vintage WWI uniforms with the real helmets.

Listening to Handel's Messiah

Greg Wilbur

Messiah (1742) by George Frideric Handel is probably the best-known work of the Baroque era—even among people who generally do not know much about Art Music. There are many helpful guides available concerning the writing and context for this musical work that go into greater detail than we are able to do so here. However, despite its familiarity, following are some points and guides to help deepen your ability to listen and more keenly hear this great masterpiece.

The Baroque Period (1600-1750) was an era of music that sought to convey emotion through expression and compelling musical devices. This impulse was a reaction to the austerity of renaissance music and led to the development of dramatic music—namely opera and oratorios. *Messiah* is an oratorio, which means it is essentially an un-staged opera usually on a religious subject. The music in an oratorio is divided into three types—choruses, recitatives, and airs (songs). The choral movements (or sections) utilize the entire choir to proclaim the text and echo it back and forth between the different voices. The other two types of music in an oratorio are for solo voices (or sometimes duets). A recitative is a "recitation" of words that are often narrative. A recitative is more text-driven than melodic. In contrast, the airs, or songs, are expressive solos that take more time to reflect on the surrounding texts in a more personal manner.

Baroque composers recognized a clear and direct connection between language and music. At its most basic level, this connection results in moments of text painting—the music actually reflecting or conveying the text. For example, the third movement (or musical section) is the tenor air on the text "Every Valley Shall Be Exalted." A number of times when the tenor sings the word "exalted," he sings with a long string of notes that sonically embellishes, or exalts, the word to reflect the meaning of the word. When he sings "hill made low," the final note of the phrase is a lower note. And when he sings "the crooked straight," the melody goes from jagged to smooth. The melodic line "paints" the actual text he is singing.

As you listen to the choral movements, notice the similarity of the melodies as each vocal part sings the same lines. Each entrance of the text in the different vocal parts is set to musical ideas that reflect each other—often either the same notes in a different octave (which are the same but higher or lower) or the same pattern of notes going up and down. Follow this melodic idea in the choral movement "And the Glory." The altos start this movement with the melody line as follows:

down-up-down-down-up-same-up-up

Immediately, the basses sing the exact same line an octave lower. The sopranos and tenors sing the same rhythm but with slight variations to the pattern of notes. Listen for how this text is sung every time—the same basic melodic idea and essentially the same pattern of notes.

As the text adds the line, "and all flesh shall see it together," the voices begin calling to one another to see the glory of the Lord until the voice are singing the word "together" at the same time. The togetherness of the text is reflected by the unity of the voices.

You can apply this type of listening to the entirety of *Messiah*, which is why it is helpful to have a copy of the text at hand while you listen, as you do in Cindy's Listening Schedule—even better would be a copy of the vocal score (the book with the music and text that a choir member would use). There are versions on-line for free, or print versions are often affordable as well.

Here are some other highlights from this week's listening:

- In "Thus Saith the Lord," the melodic line moves back and forth on the word "shake."
- "The People that Walked in Darkness" contains a roving melodic line with accidentals that sounds like someone groping in the dark for the right path.
- In "For Unto Us a Child is Born," listen for the difference in text when the chorus sings together and when they echo parts back and forth.

Cindy's Listening Schedule

Day 1
(11 minutes)

Scripture Reading

Isaiah 40:1-5

1 Comfort ye, comfort ye my people, saith your God.

2 Speak ye comfortably to Jerusalem, and cry unto her, that her warfare is accomplished, that her iniquity is pardoned: for she hath received of the Lord's hand double for all her sins.

3 The voice of him that crieth in the wilderness, Prepare ye the way of the Lord, make straight in the desert a highway for our God.

4 Every valley shall be exalted, and every mountain and hill shall be made low: and the crooked shall be made straight, and the rough places plain:

5 And the glory of the Lord shall be revealed, and all flesh shall see it together: for the mouth of the Lord hath spoken it.

Listening

Messiah Part I

No. 1. Symphony

> *(Instrumental)*

No. 2. Recitative (Tenor) "Comfort Ye..."

> *Comfort ye, comfort ye my people, saith your God.*
> *Speak ye comfortably to Jerusalem, and cry unto her, that her warfare is accomplished, that her iniquity is pardoned.*
> *The voice of him that crieth in the wilderness; prepare ye the way of the Lord; make straight in the desert a highway for our God.*
>
> *(Isaiah 40:1-3)*

No. 3.   Air (Tenor) "Every Valley..."

> *Ev'ry valley shall be exalted, and ev'ry moutain and hill made*
> *low; the crooked straight and the rough places plain.*
> (Isaiah 40:4)

No. 4.   Chorus "And the Glory ..."

> *And the glory of the Lord shall be revealed, and all flesh shall see*
> *it together: for the mouth of the Lord hath spoken it.*
> (Isaiah 40:5)

Day 2
(6½ minutes)

Scripture Reading

Haggai 2:6-7

6 For thus saith the Lord of hosts; Yet once, it is a little while, and I will shake the heavens, and the earth, and the sea, and the dry land;

7 And I will shake all nations, and the desire of all nations shall come: and I will fill this house with glory, saith the Lord of hosts.

Malachi 3:1-3

1 Behold, I will send my messenger, and he shall prepare the way before me: and the Lord, whom ye seek, shall suddenly come to his temple, even the messenger of the covenant, whom ye delight in: behold, he shall come, saith the Lord of hosts.

2 But who may abide the day of his coming? and who shall stand when he appeareth? for he is like a refiner's fire, and like fullers' soap:

3 And he shall sit as a refiner and purifier of silver: and he shall purify the sons of Levi, and purge them as gold and silver, that they may offer unto the Lord an offering in righteousness.

Listening

No. 5.   Recitative (Bass) "Thus saith the Lord..."

> *Thus saith the Lord, the Lord of hosts: Yet once a little while*

*and I will shake the heavens and the earth, the sea and the dry
land.*

*And I will shake all nations; and the desire of all nations shall
come.*

(Haggai 2:6-7)

*The Lord, whom ye seek, shall suddenly come to His temple,
even the messenger of the Covenant, whom you delight in; behold,
He shall come, saith the Lord of hosts.*

(Malachi 3:1)

No. 6.   Air (Bass) "But who may abide…"

*But who may abide the day of His coming, and who shall stand
when He appeareth? For He is like a refiner's fire.*

(Malachi 3:2)

No. 7.   Chorus "And he shall purify…"

*And He shall purify the sons of Levi, that they may offer unto
the Lord an offering in righteousness.*

(Malachi 3:3)

Day 3
(6 minutes)

Scripture Reading

Isaiah 7:14

14 Therefore the Lord himself shall give you a sign; Behold, a
virgin shall conceive, and bear a son, and shall call his name Im-
manuel.

Isaiah 40:9

9 O Zion, that bringest good tidings, get thee up into the high
mountain; O Jerusalem, that bringest good tidings, lift up thy voice
with strength; lift it up, be not afraid; say unto the cities of Judah,
Behold your God!

Isaiah 60:1

Arise, shine; for thy light is come, and the glory of the Lord is
risen upon thee.

Listening

No. 8.   Recitative (Alto) "Behold, a Virgin..."

> *Behold, a virgin shall conceive and bear a son, and shall call His name Emmanuel, God with us.*
> *(Isaiah 7:14; Matthew 1:23)*

No. 9.   Air (Alto) "O, thou that tellest..." and Chorus "Arise, Shine..."

> *O thou that tellest good tidings to Zion,*
> *get thee up into the high mountain.*
> *O thou that tellest good tidings to Jerusalem,*
> *lift up thy voice with strength;*
> *lift it up, be not afraid;*
> *say unto the cities of Judah, behold your God!*
> *(Isaiah 40: 9)*

> *O thou that tellest good tidings to Zion,*
> *arise, say unto the cities of Judah,*
> *behold your God! behold!*
> *the glory of the Lord is risen upon thee*
> *(Isaiah 40:9; 60:1)*

Day 4
(10 minutes)

Scripture Reading

Isaiah 60:2-3

2 For, behold, the darkness shall cover the earth, and gross darkness the people: but the Lord shall arise upon thee, and his glory shall be seen upon thee.

3 And the Gentiles shall come to thy light, and kings to the brightness of thy rising.

Isaiah 9:2

2 The people that walked in darkness have seen a great light: they that dwell in the land of the shadow of death, upon them hath the light shined.

Isaiah 9:6

6 For unto us a child is born, unto us a son is given: and the government shall be upon his shoulder: and his name shall be called Wonderful, Counsellor, The mighty God, The everlasting Father, The Prince of Peace.

Listening

No. 10. Recitative (Bass) "For behold, darkness…"

> *For behold, darkness shall cover the earth, and gross darkness the people; but the Lord shall arise upon thee, and His glory shall be seen upon thee.*
>
> *And the Gentiles shall come to thy light, and kings to the brightness of thy rising.*
>
> *(Isaiah 60:2-3)*

No. 11. Air (Bass) "The people who walked in darkness…"

> *The people that walked in darkness have seen a great light; and they that dwell in the land of the shadow of death, upon them hath the light shined. (Isaiah 9:2)*

No. 12. Chorus: "For unto us…"

> *For unto us a child is born, unto us a son is given, and the government shall be upon His shoulder; and His name shall be called Wonderful, Counsellor, the mighty God, the Everlasting Father, the Prince of Peace. (Isaiah 9:6)*

Day 5
(8 Minutes)

Scripture Reading

Luke 2:8-14

8 And there were in the same country shepherds abiding in the field, keeping watch over their flock by night.

9 And, lo, the angel of the Lord came upon them, and the glory of the Lord shone round about them: and they were sore afraid.

10 And the angel said unto them, Fear not: for, behold, I bring you good tidings of great joy, which shall be to all people.

11 For unto you is born this day in the city of David a Saviour, which is Christ the Lord.

12 And this shall be a sign unto you; Ye shall find the babe wrapped in swaddling clothes, lying in a manger.

13 And suddenly there was with the angel a multitude of the heavenly host praising God, and saying,

14 Glory to God in the highest, and on earth peace, good will toward men.

Listening

No. 13.   Pifa: Instrumental

No. 14.   Recitative (Soprano) "There were shepherds..."[2]

> *There were shepherds abiding in the field, keeping watch over their flocks by night.*
> *(Luke 2:8)*

No. 15.   Recitative (Soprano) "And, Lo, the angel..." and Recitative (Soprano)" And the angel said..."

> *And lo, the angel of the Lord came upon them, and the glory of the Lord shone round about them, and they were sore afraid.*
> *(Luke 2:9)*
> *And the angel said unto them: "Fear not, for behold, I bring you good tidings of great joy, which shall be to all people.*
> *For unto you is born this day in the city of David a Saviour, which is Christ the Lord."*
> *(Luke 2:10-11)*

No. 16.   Recitative (Soprano) "And suddenly..."

> *And suddenly there was with the angel, a multitude of the heavenly host, praising God, and saying:*
> *(Luke 2:13)*

---

2   Many recordings include Nos. 14-16 in one track.

No. 17. Chorus "Glory to God in the highest..."

> *"Glory to God in the highest, and peace on earth, good will towards men."*
> *(Luke 2:14)*

Day 6
(4 minutes)

Scripture Reading

Zechariah 9:9-10

9 Rejoice greatly, O daughter of Zion; shout, O daughter of Jerusalem: behold, thy King cometh unto thee: he is just, and having salvation; lowly, and riding upon an ass, and upon a colt the foal of an ass.

10 And I will cut off the chariot from Ephraim, and the horse from Jerusalem, and the battle bow shall be cut off: and he shall speak peace unto the heathen: and his dominion shall be from sea even to sea, and from the river even to the ends of the earth.

Listening

No. 18. Air (Soprano) "Rejoice greatly..."

> *Rejoice greatly, O daughter of Zion; shout, O daughter of Jerusalem!*
> *Behold, thy King cometh unto thee; He is the righteous Saviour, and He shall speak peace unto the heathen.*
> *Rejoice greatly. . . da capo*
> *(Zechariah 9:9-10)*

How Our Family Celebrates

Kerry Williamson

When I was around 8 or 9 years old, my mother purchased a felt Advent calendar. It was a cute green Christmas tree on a red background. Below it were 24 numbered pouches, each with a Velcro-backed felt ornament. I remember the excitement of getting to move each of those ornaments onto the felt tree, especially as we got to number 22 and 23 and 24! We did this for a few years, and then I suppose I got "too big" for a felt calendar, at least in my mother's mind, maybe in mine, too. As my husband and I began our family, those memories and the fact that we attended a "liturgical" church pushed me to really consider how we would observe Advent, Christmas and Epiphany with my family. We wanted to establish traditions that would honor our family's heritage (both sides) and would enrich our understanding of God's story of redemption.

We've tried, some years more successfully than others, to bring our liturgical life into our home and make more connections between Church and home. Here are some ways we have found that worked for our family.

Advent

Advent is more than just "counting down the days," although there is some aspect of this. Advent reminds us of the Jews waiting for their Messiah's appearance and encourages us as we await the Second Advent. An Advent wreath, which we have used, is a good place to start. You can easily find ideas for these all over the internet. But there are other ways I've found to set the stage for Advent and Christmas. In fact, ours unfold around the house slowly.

We begin on the first Sunday of Advent by putting out the nativity. Some years I have tried having Mary and Joseph "travel" around the house, getting closer and closer to the crèche every few days. We pull out all our Christmas books and read one together most days. Last year we read "A Christmas Carol" together. I've collected (on YouTube and Spotify) several Advent playlists, so at least while we are at home, we can enjoy these beautiful, anticipatory songs. (I cave in the car and enjoy the popular radio Christmas music!)

St. Nicholas does not come on Christmas for us, he comes on his feast day, December 6th. We celebrate with a festal breakfast and our shoes by the fireplace filled with little goodies. There are usually chocolate Santas and sometimes even some "gold" coins (Sacagawea dollars), plus a small gift. Our collection of St. Nicholas figures appears on the mantel with some twinkle lights. Sometimes we play "secret Santa" for a day or two trying to do secret good deeds for one another.

St. Lucia arrives next on December 13th. Because her name means "light," we generally put up our tree with only the lights. This is an important celebration for my husband's Swedish family, and we enjoy some Scandinavian treats to celebrate. Our traditional Scandinavian straw decorations are added to the house decorations. If our schedule allows, I especially love the tradition of a candlelight breakfast in the wee hours.

A few days before Christmas Eve, we pull out all the rest of the house decorations—including the outdoor decorations. The anticipation really starts to build now!

On Christmas Eve, we enjoy a festive family dinner, attend church, and take turns stuffing stockings. Even the kids get into the act! This is also when we pull out all the ornaments and decorate the tree. This tradition started by accident during a very busy Advent season, and it was such a fun event that we kept it. Usually grandparents are here, so they enjoy this, too. Of course, you don't have to wait until Christmas Eve, but maybe waiting until the kids are done with their school work for the semester, college kids arrive home, or another family milestone might make sense. Some people decorate on Gaudete Sunday (the third Sunday of Advent).[3]

The abandonment of Advent by many churches seems to have left a vacuum that must be filled with something. Of course, the advertisers have filled it with all manner of things. I encourage you—if you think Advent is just too much, reconsider. If you've never celebrated or kept Advent before, start simply. If you've done it for many years, scale down if you must. But don't miss it. It is a season of quiet joy and expectation. You'll find that it properly places Christmas at the pinnacle of the season rather than on a precipice.

Christmas

Christmas has positively exploded upon us now! Our Christmas celebration is not much different than most. There are goodies and decorations and Christmas songs and gifts everywhere. Because Santa has already visited our home, we can focus a bit more on Christ's birth as the source of our joy and gift-giving. We make a point of keeping our tree and exterior lights burning through all Twelve Days of Christmas (December 25th-January 5th). I try to reserve a few of our favorite Christmas movies and books for the

3   Gaudete Sunday marks the halfway point between the first Sunday of Advent and Christmas day. Advent wreath candles for the third Sunday are pink to signify the joy of being halfway to Christmas. "Gaudete" means "rejoice" in Latin.

Twelve Days. We also look for "Christmas-y" events that we can enjoy as a family after Christmas (a local gingerbread contest, is a favorite).

Perhaps you've heard of the Advent Conspiracy campaign? An even more important and counter-cultural campaign would be a Christmas Conspiracy. Instead of celebrating for one day, we'd blow the world away by celebrating a full 12-day Christmas season! Can you imagine it: Keeping a real preparatory Advent and then letting Christmas burst forth on the 25th, burning brightly for 12 whole days of delight and merriment! Sharing our tables and homes with all those we can. Giving gifts from the heart to those we love and those we don't even know. Serving our families and communities. A celebration conspiracy!

Epiphany

Epiphany, January 6th, marks the end of the Christmas season, and commemorates the visit of the Wise Men or Magi to the Christ Child. We also recognize this as a season that looks forward to the Gospel being shared with the whole world.

A lovely way to celebrate Epiphany is with a traditional home blessing and a "door chalking." Walk through your home praying over each room's occupants and activities. Then make the marks on your front door: 20+C+M+B+21 (for 2021, for example). Each person can write a small part of that, or you can let an adult write the whole thing with the kids each making their own small cross somewhere on the door. The C, M, and B traditionally stands for the legendary names of the Magi (Caspar, Melchior, and Balthazaar). However, I like the alternate: *Christus Mansionem Benedicat* which means "May Christ bless this dwelling." We don't wash off the marks, and they've stayed up as a reminder almost all year long that our home has been marked for Christ.

Perhaps end your "tour" in the kitchen or dining room with a candlelight dinner, tea or dessert of Three Kings' Cake.[4]

There have been many years that have been so busy and full (both of happy and sad events) that the thought of pulling out all the Advent/Christmas/Epiphany items, thoughtfully planning our activities, and keeping up with our various celebrations just seemed too much. We needed normalcy. But then I'd remember that those celebrations and traditions are just that.

That is one thing I appreciate about the liturgical year—when it becomes a part of your family culture, it can have a stabilizing effect. As life swirls around us, we have the familiarity of the same activities, traditions, smells, sounds, and words to keep us anchored. And what better to be anchored to than the Church, the Bride of Christ and, as the Bride of Christ, to Christ himself?

---

4   Kerry's Epiphany recipes are on page 135-137.

Week 2:
Remembering Place

Remembering Place

This week is traditionally a time to think about David's city and the prophecies surrounding this little, yet mighty, city of Bethlehem. We can also use it to think about our own place in the world and in Christ. The *Messiah* selections this week are gloomy and sorrowing. Sometimes we weep.

But it is also a time to ramp up the celebrating. Some of the angst we felt about celebrating Christmas too early has past. You cannot turn on the radio without hearing some of the worst Christmas music ever written. I don't even dare name these awful songs lest they wriggle into your ear and ruin the whole week! From Rudolph's strange antics, to maudlin made-for-TV songs, to dating nightmares, Christmas inspires songwriters everywhere to go for that royalty check. Sure, we can't help responding with our theology and philosophy when these songs start to play, but sometimes it's best just to sing along—and maybe even dance.

Advent Hymn

Come, Thou Long Expected Jesus

CHARLES WESLEY

Here we have a slightly more modern Advent hymn written in 1745 by Charles Wesley, the co-founder of Methodism and brother of John Wesley. Charles himself wrote over 6,000 hymns, many of which we still sing and love today, including "Hark, the Herald Angels Sing," another of my favorite Christmas carols.

Come, Thou long-expected Jesus,
Born to set Thy people free;
From our fears and sins release us,
Let us find our rest in Thee.
Israel's Strength and Consolation,
Hope of all the earth Thou art;
Dear Desire of every nation,
Joy of every longing heart.

Born Thy people to deliver,
Born a child and yet a King,
Born to reign in us forever,
Now Thy gracious kingdom bring.
By Thine own eternal Spirit
Rule in all our hearts alone;
By Thine all sufficient merit,
Raise us to Thy glorious throne.

This is also a good week to sing all those Advent songs about Bethlehem: "O, Little Town of Bethlehem," "Once in David's Royal City," "O, Sing a Song of Bethlehem."

Advent Scripture Memory

This passage is something every family should memorize. If you do decide to memorize this it will probably take you the entire season and you will have to learn the other passages on other years. I like the King James Version for this. Remember, children love to recite strange words. There is something very poetic about this passage.

Luke 2:1-20

1 And it came to pass in those days, that there went out a decree from Caesar Augustus that all the world should be taxed.

2 (And this taxing was first made when Cyrenius was governor of Syria.)

3 And all went to be taxed, every one into his own city.

4 And Joseph also went up from Galilee, out of the city of Nazareth, into Judaea, unto the city of David, which is called Bethlehem; (because he was of the house and lineage of David:)

5 To be taxed with Mary his espoused wife, being great with child.

6 And so it was, that, while they were there, the days were accomplished that she should be delivered.

7 And she brought forth her firstborn son, and wrapped him in swaddling clothes, and laid him in a manger; because there was no room for them in the inn.

8 And there were in the same country shepherds abiding in the field, keeping watch over their flock by night.

9 And, lo, the angel of the Lord came upon them, and the glory of the Lord shone round about them: and they were sore afraid.

10 And the angel said unto them, Fear not: for, behold, I bring you good tidings of great joy, which shall be to all people.

11 For unto you is born this day in the city of David a Saviour, which is Christ the Lord.

12 And this shall be a sign unto you; Ye shall find the babe wrapped in swaddling clothes, lying in a manger.

13 And suddenly there was with the angel a multitude of the heavenly host praising God, and saying,

14 Glory to God in the highest, and on earth peace, good will toward men.

15 And it came to pass, as the angels were gone away from them into heaven, the shepherds said one to another, Let us now go even unto Bethlehem, and see this thing which is come to pass, which the Lord hath made known unto us.

16 And they came with haste, and found Mary, and Joseph, and the babe lying in a manger.

17 And when they had seen it, they made known abroad the saying which was told them concerning this child.

18 And all they that heard it wondered at those things which were told them by the shepherds.

19 But Mary kept all these things, and pondered them in her heart.

20 And the shepherds returned, glorifying and praising God for all the things that they had heard and seen, as it was told unto them.

Advent Poetry

In keeping with our aim to have fun this week, we read Shakespeare's poem "Winter," from the closing scene of Love's Labour Lost.

Winter

WILLIAM SHAKESPEARE

When icicles hang by the wall,
 And Dick the shepherd blows his nail,
And Tom bears logs into the hall,
  And milk comes frozen home in pail;
When blood is nipp'd, and ways be foul,
Then nightly sings the staring owl,
      Tu-whit, to-who!—

A merry note,
While greasy Joan doth keel the pot.

When all aloud the wind doth blow,
 And coughing drowns the parson's saw,
And birds sit brooding in the snow,
   And Marian's nose looks red and raw;
When roasted crabs hiss in the bowl,
Then nightly sings the staring owl,
                    Tu-whit, to-who!—
A merry note,
While greasy Joan doth keel the pot.

Advent Feast Day

St. Lucia's Day - December 13

This feast day originally fell, in the Julian calendar, on the winter solstice. Today it is celebrated on December 13. Christians used this time of darkness to celebrate the coming of the Light which begins as the days grow longer after the solstice. You may remember seeing pictures of pretty Swedish girls, walking in white robes tied with red sashes, wearing wreaths of candles on their heads. It is hard to suggest to modern mommas that this might be a good idea. Still, it is a very pretty feast day.

St. Lucia herself was a third-century martyr who brought food to Christians hiding in the dark catacombs. In order to free up her hands to carry more food, she wore a wreath of candles to light her way. Much of this story is unsubstantiated, but it is a beautiful feast day to celebrate the end of darkness and the coming of light. St. Lucia's Day is traditionally celebrated by Catholics and Lutherans. Even though Lucia was Sicilian, the holiday is essentially Swedish and depictions of St. Lucia look more Nordic than Sicilian.

My own mother, who knew nothing of St. Lucia, often made a Swedish tea ring for coffee klatches. These were gatherings of local women in the 1960s and 1970s. I still remember the lovely smell of her percolated coffee and yeast rolls. Many Swedish tea ring recipes are in fact called St. Lucia's Crown. My mom's recipe is on page 122.

Just for Fun

Don't forget to intersperse some rollicking modern songs into your celebrations. "Rockin' Around the Christmas Tree," "Rudolf the Red-Nosed Reindeer," and "Jingle Bells," can make the many extra holiday chores more fun.

Our family loves Mannheim Steamroller. One Christmas we took our two oldest boys to a Mannheim Steamroller concert in Philadelphia. I could not have been more than six months pregnant with someone that December (I can't remember now who), but I felt full-term huge, and our tickets were for the upper level of the arena. We had trudged all the way up to the top when an official came up to us with good news. We had been selected to sit at the tables, filled with food and drink, on the floor of the arena very close to the band! It was a magical night to remember. We always decorate our tree with Mannheim Steamroller as our soundtrack!

> Don't forget to intersperse some rollicking modern songs into your celebrations.

Perhaps your children are in holiday plays and programs at this time. If you have recitation nights with other families, Christmas is a great theme and a good excuse for a party. For years, my husband used to sing with the children. One of the best songs they did was a Judy Rogers song called "Listen My Son." One year, we signed up to sing at our church's Christmas Open House program during the local historical tour of homes. We decided to sing a Twila Paris medley "White Christmas/Whiter than Snow." My husband was unable to attend. We sang so badly that day that we never sang in public again, although we did do a very nice harmonic "Silver Bells" in the van when traveling.

Reminder: Start looking around for a local production or sing-along of the *Messiah*. They are often earlier in the season than expected. You can also look around for local Lessons and Carols services.[5]

5   I write more about Lessons and Carols services in "Advent Feast: Christmas Eve" on page 94.

Listening to Handel's Messiah

Greg Wilbur

George Frideric Handel (1685-1759) was from Halle, Germany, but he made his fame and fortune in London primarily writing operas and oratorios for concert performances. He was quite popular and revered but found further acclaim with his instrumental works for royalty—*Music for the Royal Fireworks* (1749) and *Water Music* (1717) which was played on a barge for King George I on the river Thames. In 1727 he composed the choral anthem *Zadok the Priest* for the coronation of George II and it has been sung at every coronation since. He wrote more than 40 operas in little more than 30 years.

Handel was so popular in London that at his death he was buried in Westminster Abbey in Poet's Corner with full state honors. The fact that much of his career and writing was in London has two relevant points with regard to the *Messiah*—the original language is English and it was written as a concert work and not for liturgical/worship purposes. That does not diminish the beauty of the work but rather gives context for the aesthetics and structure of the piece.

Messiah is divided into three main parts. Part 1 covers the prophetic anticipation of the first coming of the Christ and the birth of Jesus. Part 2 begins with "Behold the Lamb of God" and transitions to the work of Christ specifically in the events of Passion Week—betrayal, punishment, and crucifixion. Part 3 builds on the fact that

"He shall reign forever and ever" to give us the assurance of the death of death and the second coming of Christ.

Here are some things to listen for from this week's selections:

- "He Shall Feed His Flock" has the same feel as the Pastoral Symphony. This is an expressive device used by Handel (and others) to use the form of a "pastoral" in setting a text dealing with flocks and shepherds. It is intended to evoke a rustic and rural locale with a mood that matches the peace and rest promised in the lyrics.
- "His Yoke is Easy, and His Burthen is Light" presents an aural representation of lightness and an easy burden. Notice how Handel achieves that effect.
- "And With His Stripes We are Healed" presents a single line of text repeated more than 20 times which simultaneously reminds us of the incessant, painful lashing of Christ but also the depths and cost of the healing that He brings. With the music for "All We Like Sheep," the music wanders in the likeness of sheep who have gone astray. When the text moves to "And the Lord has laid on Him the iniquity of us all," the character of the music changes to more chromatic and dissonant notes to reflect the weight of our transgressions.
- The derision and mocking of those surrounding Christ on the cross comes through the challenge and antagonism inherent in the choral lines as they sing "He Trusted in God That He Would Deliver Him."

Cindy's Listening Schedule

Day 7
(7 minutes)

Scripture Reading

<u>Isaiah 35:5-6</u>

5 Then the eyes of the blind shall be opened, and the ears of the deaf shall be unstopped.

6 Then shall the lame man leap as an hart, and the tongue of the dumb sing: for in the wilderness shall waters break out, and streams in the desert.

<u>Isaiah 40:11</u>

11 He shall feed his flock like a shepherd: he shall gather the lambs with his arm, and carry them in his bosom, and shall gently lead those that are with young.

<u>Matthew 11:28-30</u>

28 Come unto me, all ye that labour and are heavy laden, and I will give you rest.

29 Take my yoke upon you, and learn of me; for I am meek and lowly in heart: and ye shall find rest unto your souls.

30 For my yoke is easy, and my burden is light.

Listening

No. 19.   Recitative (Alto) "Then shall the eyes of the blind..."

Then shall the eyes of the blind be opened, and the ears of the deaf unstopped.
Then shall the lame man leap as an hart, and the tongue of the dumb shall sing.
(Isaiah 35:5-6)

No. 20. Aria (Alto) "He shall feed..." and "Come unto me..."

> *He shall feed His flock like a shepherd; and He shall gather the lambs with His arm, and carry them in His bosom, and gently lead those that are with young.*
> *(Isaiah 40:11)*

> *Come unto Him, all ye that labour, come unto Him that are heavy laden, and He will give you rest.*
> *Take his yoke upon you, and learn of Him, for He is meek and lowly of heart, and ye shall find rest unto your souls.*
> *(Matthew 11:28-29)*

No. 21. Chorus "His yoke is easy..."

> *His yoke is easy, and His burden is light.*
> *(Matthew 11:30)*

Day 8
(3 minutes)

Messiah Part 2

Scripture Reading

John 1:29

29 The next day John seeth Jesus coming unto him, and saith, Behold the Lamb of God, which taketh away the sin of the world.

Listening

No. 22. Chorus "Behold the Lamb..."

> *Behold the Lamb of God, that taketh away the sin of the world.*
> *(John 1:29)*

Day 9
(11 minutes)

Scripture Reading

Isaiah 53:3

3 He is despised and rejected of men; a man of sorrows, and acquainted with grief: and we hid as it were our faces from him; he was despised, and we esteemed him not.

Isaiah 53:6

6 All we like sheep have gone astray; we have turned every one to his own way; and the Lord hath laid on him the iniquity of us all.

Listening

No. 23.   Air (Alto) "He was despised..."

> *He was despised and rejected of men, a man of sorrows and acquainted with grief.*
> *(Isaiah 53:3)*

> *He gave His back to the smiters, and His cheeks to them that plucked off His hair: He hid not His face from shame and spitting. He was despised. . . da capo*
> *(Isaiah 53:6)*

Day 10
(7 minutes)

Scripture Reading

Isaiah 53:4-6

4 Surely he hath borne our griefs, and carried our sorrows: yet we did esteem him stricken, smitten of God, and afflicted.

5 But he was wounded for our transgressions, he was bruised for our iniquities: the chastisement of our peace was upon him; and with his stripes we are healed.

6 All we like sheep have gone astray; we have turned every one to his own way; and the Lord hath laid on him the iniquity of us all.

Listening

No. 24.   Chorus "Surely he hath borne…"

> *Surely He hath borne our griefs, and carried our sorrows!*
> *He was wounded for our transgressions, He was bruised for our*
> *iniquities; the chastisement of our peace was upon Him.*
> *(Isaiah 53:4-5)*

No. 25.   Chorus "And with his stripes…"

> *And with His stripes we are healed.*
> *(Isaiah 53:5)*

No. 26.   Chorus "All we like sheep…"

> *All we like sheep have gone astray; we have turned every one to*
> *his own way. And the Lord hath laid on Him the iniquity of us all.*
> *(Isaiah 53:6)*

Day 11
(3 minutes)

Scripture Reading

Psalm 22:7-8

7 All they that see me laugh me to scorn: they shoot out the lip, they shake the head, saying,

8 He trusted on the Lord that he would deliver him: let him deliver him, seeing he delighted in him.

Listening

No. 27.   Recitative (Tenor) "All they that see him laugh…"
> *All they that see Him laugh Him to scorn; they shoot out their*
> *lips, and shake their heads, saying:*
> *(Psalm 22:7)*

No. 28.   Chorus "He trusted in God…"

> *"He trusted in God that He would deliver Him; let Him deliver*
> *Him, if He delight in Him."*
> *(Psalm 22:8)*

61

Day 12
(4 minutes)

Scripture Reading

<u>Psalm 69:20</u>

20 Reproach hath broken my heart; and I am full of heaviness: and I looked for some to take pity, but there was none; and for comforters, but I found none.

<u>Lamentations 1:12</u>

12 Is it nothing to you, all ye that pass by? behold, and see if there be any sorrow like unto my sorrow, which is done unto me, wherewith the Lord hath afflicted me in the day of his fierce anger.

Listening

No. 29.   Recitative (Soprano) "Thy rebuke has broken..."

Thy rebuke hath broken His heart: He is full of heaviness. He looked for some to have pity on Him, but there was no man, neither found He any to comfort him.
(Psalm 69:20)

No. 30.   Arioso (Soprano) "Behold and see if..."

Behold, and see if there be any sorrow like unto His sorrow.
(Lamentations 1:12)

How Our Family Celebrates

Lynn Bruce

The angelic host has descended once again. A myriad lot they are, variously made from the plunder of my crafty children: clothespins, yarn, cotton balls, buttons, raffia, toilet paper tubes, Daddy's new socks. I carry them down from the attic gingerly and unpack them with fear and trembling because these are the Christmas decorations I cannot replace. They are my favorites nowadays because time is a healer and I no longer clearly recall the catastrophic fiats of their creation. I was young then and given to much sweeping because somewhere it is written that angels dwell in glorious light which my clever children transliterated as glitter. And glory shone around, for sure.

My children's capacity for Christmas traditions was a thing of wonder and fable. The glitterpalooza at our kitchen table was just a warmup. Every Christmas they conjured up some new mode of merriment and promptly declared it an annual happening henceforth and anon. Their father would chide them in his Statler & Waldorf voice: "We did it once—it's a tradition!" Children being literalists, they apparently mistook his joke for a definition. We absolutely had to do the Muppet Christmas Carol quote-along, the caroling ride through the neighborhood with the car windows down and the heater up, the toy train exhibit at the mall, the Twelve Days of Christmas stroll through the botanical gardens—and of course the customary flurry of baking, singing, wrapping, and steadily escalating glee. Eventually our household agenda for all the food and fun slated for Christmas Eve and Christmas Adam (which is the day before Christmas Eve, naturally) required flow charts. Poster-sized. Taped to the kitchen wall. I am not kidding. Please note that I drew the line at celebrating a day called Christmas Cain.

Regardless of when our tree went up, the season truly began the day I hauled the Christmas books out of storage. It was like changing the channel—suddenly the language of the house shifted and Christmas was on the air. Since I always had the day shift in the read-aloud chair, Dad was the purveyor of bedtime stories. He spent many December evenings reading aloud to a vacant sofa because our kids found it more elfin to listen behind the Christmas tree. Certain books were like old friends who only come round to visit in December: *The Gift of the Magi* by O. Henry, *A Christmas Carol* by Charles Dickens, and always *The Story of Santa Claus* by Scribbler Elf. We all have particularly fond memories of *The Christmas Mystery* by Jostein Gaarder, an Advent pilgrimage tale which travels in reverse through time, space, and human history all the way back to the manger in Bethlehem. To this book I owe the priceless memory of witnessing my dear husband in jolly elf pajamas earnestly explaining the world to a tree.

Family traditions can give us a soft place to land in hard times.

Family traditions can give us a soft place to land in hard times. I learned this first from my grandmother. Mema had a life so hard it breaks my heart, but she understood the overcoming power of a family celebrating, feasting, remembering, rejoicing in the goodness of God together. She grew up on the rim of the Dust Bowl in Oklahoma and came of age in the Great Depression. She learned young to scavenge the beauty at hand all year long in anticipation of Christmas. She and her sisters saved bits of used kitchen foil to scrunch into shiny stars, and collected empty Vick's jars made of pretty cobalt glass with bright green lids—my father remembered her hanging these on the tree when he was a boy. Little more was needed to keep

Christmas: the family Bible, a hymnal, firewood, and love. I only knew Mema after long heartache and trauma had bridled her joy. But even in a marriage hindered by chronic sin, she kept a strong sense of family and heritage alive almost singlehandedly in a way that still matters for her descendants of my children's generation who never knew her. Memory is redemptive, a healer. At Christmas, Mema remembered the light which darkness could not apprehend, and her heart was lifted. She was once again that Oklahoma girl scavenging all the beauty she could find. Her eyes danced like a child's. Mema at Christmas was buoyant and playful, and all her tribe followed suit. This was us at our best. It was beautiful.

> Memory is redemptive, a healer. At Christmas, Mema remembered the light which darkness could not apprehend, and her heart was lifted.

Mema never knew my children, but she inspired me to be playful with them. To this I owe my favorite days of mothering. Like the time I dragged our mattresses into the living room for a family slumber party. The time my children awoke to sheets tenting the whole den for a week of "campschooling." The days I wrote the children tiny letters, in the guise of an alter ego, which were delivered by a fairy sparrow to tin can mailboxes—and got tiny letters back from the likes of Laura Ingalls, Elizabeth Bennett, and various tank engines. Sometimes we made a game of sneaking curious lumps into one another's stockings all through December—an orange, a ping-pong ball, a small jar of buttons. In my best years, a bustling miniature snow village magically appeared overnight, like Brigadoon. That year we cut a blizzard of big paper snowflakes and hung them from the living room ceiling was wonder-full, no other way to say it. What fun to see visiting friends look up and gasp, even the oldest faces easing back into childlike delight. Everyone should live in a snow dome at least once.

Neither Dan nor I inherited a tradition of observing Advent

in conventional ways, but we knew Jesus' love and we knew how to throw a feast, and for us that has turned out to be everything and enough. Our most treasured tradition we've created together is our Anniversary Tree. Every year since we married, Dan and I have added a crystal ornament to our own little tree to celebrate another year together. Even in some lean years when we barely got by, we made sure to sock away enough pocket change for our special ornament. Three decades later, our Anniversary Tree is rather like an evergreen Ebenezer of our life together. Dan jokes that it represents our net worth, and in a way he's right. Celebrating marriage is admittedly a peculiar way to observe Advent, but it strikes me as fitting. The coming of the Christ child fills us with expectation and hope because it keeps us in remembrance that He is surely coming the second time as a bridegroom for His bride. Every Christmas feast is a prelude to the great wedding feast.

> Our most treasured tradition we've created together is our Anniversary Tree.

It may well have been Handel's *Messiah* which originally planted the seed of that idea in our hearts. Soon after we became engaged, Dan and I went to a sing-along with The Dallas Bach Society, which performs the oratorio on period instruments from an original score. That was my first time to hear *Messiah* as Handel heard it, and I was captivated. Dan and I started a lovely ritual of playing it on Saturday evenings during dinner. When our children came along, we dreamed of taking them to the sing-along. Once they were good readers, I planned a fall term of learning the libretto with them. We kept it simple. Most mornings we read a section aloud and used the verses for copywork. We listened to it performed on period instruments by Christopher Hogwood and the Academy of Ancient Music. When the big day came to attend the concert, the children were ready and excited, and they sang along from start to finish! They still say that this is one of the best Christmas memories of their childhood, a formative experience that has deeply enriched their lives. It is sweet to be a family that has sung HALLELUJAH! together with all our hearts. For this we are grateful.

It is knit into children's hearts to love traditions, to crave the repetition of remembering together, of reviewing again what was and is and is to come. Surely God's fingerprints are on this. From the beginnings of times and seasons, He has asked His people to gather and feast at special times, to remember and rejoice together. Is it any wonder we feel comfort and joy in an atmosphere filled with light, singing, and the good tidings of the angels? This is rejoicing as God rejoiced. Our Christmas traditions are echoes through time, our repeat of the sounding joy that unto us a Child is given—the first and best gift. Back when it seemed my small children could only articulate that joy by making yet another glittery mess, I believe even then this was the gift their souls wanted most.

Week 3:
Remembering The People
Waiting for Christ

Remembering the People Waiting for Christ

Traditionally, the third week of Advent focuses on the shepherds who were waiting for their Messiah. You can return to Day 5 of *Messiah* (page 37) to hear many of the shepherds' songs, and last week we saw the theme of shepherding and lambs running through the work. But the shepherds were not the only people waiting on Christ. We see in Hebrews 11 that many, many people throughout history were waiting for this moment. "And what more shall I say? For time would fail me to tell of Gideon, Barak, Samson, Jephthah, of David and Samuel and the prophets" (Hebrews 11:32 ESV). When Jesus was taken to the temple to be circumcised, two very old people, Simeon and Anna, were waiting for him and recognized him. Their whole life was completed by the act of seeing the Messiah in the flesh. Now they could depart in peace.

We also are people waiting for Christ to return once again and make all things new. We, and even the creation, groan as we wait. But we know from Hebrews 12 that our waiting is not in vain, in fact, it is the stuff of faith.

"Therefore, since we are surrounded by so great a cloud of witnesses, let us also lay aside every weight, and sin which clings so closely, and let us run with endurance the race that is set before us, looking to Jesus, the founder and perfecter of our faith, who for the joy that was set before him endured the cross, despising the shame, and is seated at the right hand of the throne of God." Hebrews 12:1-2 (ESV)

As we near Christmas Day, we remember that long ago the prophecies were fulfilled and will be fulfilled again. This is why we sing the words, "O come, all ye faithful."

Advent Hymn

Here we have the traditional Christmas carol "O Come, All Ye Faithful," both in Latin ("Adestes Fidelis") and in English. I like to sing it both ways.

Adeste fideles	O come, all ye faithful,
læti triumphantes,	joyful and triumphant!
Venite, venite in Bethlehem.	O come ye, O come ye to Bethlehem;
Natum videte	Come and behold him
Regem angelorum:	Born the King of Angels:
Venite adoremus (3×)	O come, let us adore Him, (3×)
Dominum.	Christ the Lord.
Deum de Deo, lumen de lumine	God of God, light of light,
Gestant puellæ viscera	Lo, he abhors not the Virgin's womb;
Deum verum, genitum non factum.	Very God, begotten, not created:
Venite adoremus (3×)	O come, let us adore Him, (3×)
Dominum.	Christ the Lord.
Cantet nunc io, chorus angelorum;—	Sing, choirs of angels, sing in exultation,
Cantet nunc aula cælestium,	Sing, all ye citizens of Heaven above!
Gloria, gloria in excelsis Deo,	Glory to God, glory in the highest:
Venite adoremus (3×)	O come, let us adore Him, (3×)
Dominum.	Christ the Lord.
Ergo qui natus die hodierna.	Yea, Lord, we greet thee, born this happy morning;
Jesu, tibi sit gloria,	Jesus, to thee be glory given!
Patris æterni Verbum caro factum.	Word of the Father, now in flesh appearing!
Venite adoremus (3×)	O come, let us adore Him, (3×)
Dominum.	Christ the Lord.

Advent Scripture Memory

This passage about Simeon is from Luke 2. Simeon had been waiting for the Messiah because the Holy Spirit revealed to him he would not die until he saw the Lord. If you start at verse 25 you get the whole story, or you can just memorize the beautiful song of Simeon in verses 29-32 of Luke 2.

Luke 2:25-35 (ESV)

25 Now there was a man in Jerusalem, whose name was Simeon, and this man was righteous and devout, waiting for the consolation of Israel, and the Holy Spirit was upon him.

26 And it had been revealed to him by the Holy Spirit that he would not see death before he had seen the Lord's Christ.

27 And he came in the Spirit into the temple, and when the parents brought in the child Jesus, to do for him according to the custom of the Law,

28 he took him up in his arms and blessed God and said,

29 "Lord, now you are letting your servant depart in peace,
according to your word;

30 for my eyes have seen your salvation

31 that you have prepared in the presence of all peoples,

32 a light for revelation to the Gentiles,
and for glory to your people Israel."

33 And his father and his mother marveled at what was said about him.

34 And Simeon blessed them and said to Mary his mother, "Behold, this child is appointed for the fall and rising of many in Israel, and for a sign that is opposed

35 (and a sword will pierce through your own soul also), so that thoughts from many hearts may be revealed."

Advent Poetry

The Shepherd's Tale

THOMAS BANKS

We came down from the hills that night
When first we heard the voices calling
Us to the village on the plain.
The wind was low, and snow was falling.

The place was still, and with slow steps
Unsure we stumbled in the night
And saw at last, for all the starless
Dark, a dimly glowing light.

The light was shining in a cave
Set at the foot of some low hill,
And there we turned with hope to find
Warm rest against the nighttime chill.

As soon as we had stepped inside,
We knew the voices that we heard
Had led us. What we saw that night
Needs better than the stumbling word

Of my fool's tongue to tell it fair.
Let this suffice: inside we saw
The end to which my every path
By an unalterable law

Had from the first been traced that I
Might now bear witness to the same,
That men may know at last of love
And strength and truth and peace the Name.

Just for Fun

There is no feast day for this week. Perhaps it is good to take a break and begin preparing for Christmas Eve and Christmas Day themselves at this time. We like to have a cookie decorating party during this week. I like to make all my cookies over a couple of days. I make at least four kinds of cookies each year. With a large family of boys, and many friends and neighbors, it was hard to make enough cookies. I start by making sugar cookie dough and chilling it. Later, the children and I cut the cookies into shapes. We seem to like decorating Santas and Christmas trees best. I bake all of the cookies and set them on plates and trays to cool. Usually on the second day we have a decorating party—complete with prizes for the best decorated Santa, the best overall cookie, and the most original. As the years went by, this competition, like all competitions in our family, grew to ridiculous levels. I am happy to say that we have been able to keep this tradition going with our little granddaughters, Anabella and Savanna. You can find my four Christmas cookie recipes in the recipe section starting on page 124.

Here is one more idea you will probably not find in any other Advent book: a Christmas prank. With a family of many boys, keeping cookies in the house takes ingenuity and threats. It wasn't enough to say, "Stay out of the cookies." After all, what is one cookie gone among so many? It wasn't enough to freeze them, because after all, they still taste good frozen with coffee. One year, my daughter Emily and I came up with an idea when we knew the college boys were coming home. We made a couple of really, really awful cookies. We added chili pepper, onion powder, and all kinds of gross things. We set out a plate of Christmas cookies, and we told the boys NOT to eat them. It was a sweet victory watching them sputter and threaten revenge.

Listening to Handel's *Messiah*

Greg Wilbur

I n 1741–42, Handel travelled to Dublin, Ireland and put on a series of subscription concerts. While he was there he decided to premiere *Messiah* as a charity concert to raise funds for three different charitable organizations. He received permission from two churches to use their choirs for the occasion, and on April 13, 1742, seven hundred people crowded the Great Music Hall on Fishamble Street for the concert and fundraiser.

One thing to note is the size and composition of the choir—it was comprised of thirty-two singers all of whom were men or boys. The only women who sang in the performance were the soprano and alto soloists. The orchestra was also of modest size. From a performance perspective in this time period, the use of an all-male choir and small ensemble would have been quite typical. The benefit is that this allows for a light and flexible approach to the long and fast passages that the choir sings and the instruments play.

As musical tastes changed after the death of Handel, several composers re-orchestrated *Messiah* to include more instrumental parts. In addition, the lighter approach of a small ensemble was replaced by large-scale ensembles. In 1784, 525 singers and players performed *Messiah* at Westminster Abbey. A revised performance in Europe in 1788 consisted of more than 250 vocalists and an orchestra of nearly 90 strings along with a full complement of winds and brass, including seven trumpets (*five* more than Handel used) and eleven oboes (*eleven* more than Handel used). Mid-nineteenth century performances of *Messiah* in the United States included versions with 300 and 600 singers in New York and Boston.

It is easy to see why people would want to maximize the impact and power of the text and music with a matching spectacle of sight and sound; however, there is a purity and flexibility to performances that maintain an approach closer to that which Handel used. Much could be said in defense of both approaches with enjoyment in both.

As we continue this week, here are some pointers for listening:

- How does the discussion about the size of choirs influence the way you now listen to "Lift Up Your Heads, O Ye Gates," "The Lord Gave the Word," and "Their Sound is Gone Out into All Lands?" Try to listen to a couple of versions of some of these choral movements that use varying size choirs and orchestras and notice the difference that makes.

- With the Air "How Beautiful are the Feet of Them," Handel again uses a pastoral feel to evoke and connect the idea of peace to the beauty of natural settings. "Their Sound is Gone Out into All Lands" includes a rising melodic line that corresponds to the words going out to the ends of the earth.

- The idea of peace is missing musically while the nations rage and the kings of the earth rise up in the bass Air "Why Do the Nations So Furiously Rage Together." In the final listening for this week, the chorus sings "Let Us Break Their Bonds Asunder" to a broken melody that portrays the breaking of bonds and the casting away of their yokes.

Cindy's Listening Schedule

Day 13
(5 ½ minutes)

Scripture Reading

Isaiah 53:8

8 He was taken from prison and from judgment: and who shall declare his generation? for he was cut off out of the land of the living: for the transgression of my people was he stricken.

Psalm 16:10

10 For thou wilt not leave my soul in hell; neither wilt thou suffer thine Holy One to see corruption.

Psalm 24:7-10

7 Lift up your heads, O ye gates; and be ye lift up, ye everlasting doors; and the King of glory shall come in.

8 Who is this King of glory? The Lord strong and mighty, the Lord mighty in battle.

9 Lift up your heads, O ye gates; even lift them up, ye everlasting doors; and the King of glory shall come in.

10 Who is this King of glory? The Lord of hosts, he is the King of glory. Selah.

Listening

No. 31.   Recitative (Tenor or Soprano) "He was cut off..."

> *He was cut off out of the land of the living: for the transgressions of Thy people was He stricken.*
> (Isaiah 53:8)

No. 32.   Air (Tenor or Soprano) "But thou didst not leave..."

> *But Thou didst not leave His soul in hell; nor didst Thou suffer Thy Holy One to see corruption.*
> (Psalm 16:10)

No. 33. Chorus "Lift up your heads..."

> *Lift up your heads, O ye gates; and be ye lift up, ye everlasting doors; and the King of Glory shall come in.*
>
> *Who is this King of Glory? The Lord strong and mighty, The Lord mighty in battle.*
>
> *Lift up your heads, O ye gates; and be ye lift up, ye everlasting doors; and the King of Glory shall come in.*
>
> *Who is this King of Glory? The Lord of Hosts, He is the King of Glory.*
>
> *(Psalm 24:7-10)*

Day 14
(2 minutes)

Scripture Reading

Hebrews 1:5-6

5 For unto which of the angels said he at any time, Thou art my Son, this day have I begotten thee? And again, I will be to him a Father, and he shall be to me a Son?

6 And again, when he bringeth in the first begotten into the world, he saith, And let all the angels of God worship him.

Listening

No. 34. Recitative (Tenor) "Unto which of the ..."

> *Unto which of the angels said He at any time: "Thou art My Son, this day have I begotten Thee?"*
>
> *(Hebrews 1:5)*

No. 35. Chorus "Let all the angels..."

> *Let all the angels of God worship Him.*
>
> *(Hebrews 1:6)*

Day 15
(5 minutes)

Scripture Reading

Psalm 68:11

11 The Lord gave the word: great was the company of those that published it.

Psalm 68:18

18 Thou hast ascended on high, thou hast led captivity captive: thou hast received gifts for men; yea, for the rebellious also, that the Lord God might dwell among them.

Listening

No. 36.   Air (Bass, Alto or Soprano) "Thou art gone up..."

> Thou art gone up on high; Thou hast led captivity captive, and received gifts for men; yea, even from Thine enemies, that the Lord God might dwell among them.
> (Psalm 68:18)

No. 37.   Chorus "The Lord gave the word..."

> The Lord gave the word; great was the company of the preachers.
> (Psalm 68:11)

Day 16
(3 minutes)

Scripture Reading

Romans 10:15

15 And how shall they preach, except they be sent? as it is written, How beautiful are the feet of them that preach the gospel of peace, and bring glad tidings of good things!

Isaiah 52:7

7 How beautiful upon the mountains are the feet of him that bringeth good tidings, that publisheth peace; that bringeth good tidings of good, that publisheth salvation; that saith unto Zion, Thy God reigneth!

Listening

No. 38.   Duet (Soprano, Alto, Chorus) "How beautiful..."

> *How beautiful are the feet of them that preach the gospel of peace, and bring glad tidings of good things.*
> *(Isaiah 52:7; Romans 10:15)*

Day 17
(1 minute)

Scripture Reading

Romans 10:18

18 But I say, Have they not heard? Yes verily, their sound went into all the earth, and their words unto the ends of the world.

Psalm 19:4

4 Their line is gone out through all the earth, and their words to the end of the world. In them hath he set a tabernacle for the sun...

Listening

No. 39.   Arioso (Tenor) "Their sound..."

> *Their sound is gone out into all lands,*
> *and their words unto the ends of the world.*
> *(Romans 10:18; Psalm 19:4)*

Day 18
(3 minutes)

Scripture Reading

<u>Psalm 2:1-3</u>

1 Why do the heathen rage, and the people imagine a vain thing?

2 The kings of the earth set themselves, and the rulers take counsel together, against the Lord, and against his anointed, saying,

3 Let us break their bands asunder, and cast away their cords from us.

Listening

No. 40. Air (Bass) "Why do the nations..."

Why do the nations so furiously rage together, and why do the people imagine a vain thing?

The kings of the earth rise up, and the rulers take counsel together against the Lord, and against His anointed.

(Psalm 2:1-2)

No. 41. Chorus "Let us break..."

Let us break their bonds asunder, and cast away their yokes from us.

(Psalm 2:3)

A Light Shines in Darkness

Caitlin Bruce Beauchamp

Like many traditions, our annual Winter Solstice Sunset Prairie Walk came into being almost of its own accord. That particular December, winter solstice fell on the night of the full moon. Imagine: the early solstice sunset on one horizon giving way to full moonrise on the other, in the twilight of the year's longest night. Such magic is irresistible, or so you'd think, and in my dreams my family would have observed it with some gracious, meaningful celebration.

But in real life, my family—like any family, I suppose—is prone to bungled ideals and miscommunicated plans. It turned out my husband's car needed a repair, and needed it immediately, from a specific mechanic in a specific suburb, and he needed to drop it off after work, and we'd have to pick him up—and had either of us communicated our plans to the other? Well, no, we hadn't. And so that evening as the solstice sun set we were not sharing a candlelight feast or lighting a bonfire, but picking up Taco Bueno in a bedraggled industrial suburb on our way home from the mechanic. Night gathered itself together around the blisters of brightness emanating from neon signs, streetlights, and headlights. We took our sack of burritos home and, in a last attempt to honor the day, ate by candlelight.

You know how it is. These things just happen, and we shrug and laugh at ourselves and intend better things for next year. To this attitude I was wistfully resigned, but the next evening my husband suggested we try again, go watch the sunset somewhere. Why not? After all, it was only a day past solstice. The moon was still full. We bundled everyone into sweaters and hats and shoes, racing against the descending sun, and drove to the untamed city park we like to call our prairie. It's a hidden gem tucked away within a spic-and-span midcentury neighborhood; what looks like an unkempt field is actually a mostly undisturbed patch of native prairie ecosystem, a rarity in our urbanized region. Now, in the cold wind of December, it stirred and whispered with dry prairie grasses and wildflower stalks gone to seed.

> We bundled everyone into sweaters and hats and shoes, racing against the descending sun, and drove to the untamed city park we like to call our prairie.

In any season, a prairie has a smell all its own, wild, clean, and beneficent. We breathed deeply, and we watched the sun go down, a fire dying out behind the strong dark outline of cedar trees to the west. There was a lull, and one child grew fussy waiting in the twilight, and we sang carols to distract her, and then finally a brightness shimmered above the roofs of the nice respectable houses to the east. Little by little the full moon rose until there it was, all of it, in its impossible newly-risen brightness and clarity. We smiled at each other, our faces pale and luminous, turned toward the light. Somewhere far away, deep in the greenbelt at our backs, a coyote howled.

And then we went home and put our children to bed. That was all, and probably it doesn't seem like much. But I knew this was something I wanted my children to remember about Christmastime: that we took them out walking in a field at sunset on solstice, and their legs got scratched by the summer's blackberry brambles unseen in the dark, and there were coyotes. Not your typical holiday cheer, perhaps—but there is something profound in witnessing the arrival of the longest night. This is the fulcrum of Creation's year, the moment everything turns: though cold months and long nights lie ahead, already the light is returning, each day a little longer than the one before. It is a metaphor woven into the cycle of the seasons, yet another refraction of the Great Story of hope we are living here on earth.

> It is a metaphor woven into the cycle of the seasons, yet another refraction of the Great Story of hope we are living here on earth.

Thus without fanfare or forethought we gained a new Christmas tradition, one beautifully suited to our individual family: simple, rooted in nature and our specific geographical place, requiring little fuss from a mother not naturally inclined to or gifted in the preparation of elaborate festivities. Our children are young, and our holiday traditions are still forming. It's tempting in these years to feel like we must be Very Intentional about creating meaningful traditions, and yet when I deliberately try to inaugurate one, the result can sometimes seem shallow or forced. But when I keep an open hand and an observant spirit, attentive to what arises as we move through the Christmas season, our family culture of celebration unfolds organically year by year.

I grew up in a family where Christmas was joyously celebrated. Family traditions ranged from the serious to the outright silly, supported by my mother's willingness to go to the extra effort of festivity, her ability to make an occasion feel special. Now that I have my own family, we still delight to join my parents' household for the pinnacle of the season. This is where the big Christmas tree is decorated, where presents are piled up, and where Santa visits, heralded by all manner of rituals. Though we live just ten minutes away, we pack our bags and spend several nights of Christmas week staying in my parents' home. It's a wonderful change of rhythm to be together in the same house, and combining our different gifts and strengths and temperaments enriches the holiday for us all. In the days *before* Christmas, we share the cooking, last-minute preparations, favorite Christmas music and movies. In the days *after,* we savor quietness, rest, reading our new books, eating leftovers, and playing with the children. These pleasant days after Christmas are my favorites of the season.

In my own household, we've drifted toward observing Advent, in a casual, low-church, mildly disheveled sort of way. We begin the season with a walk in a nearby wooded creek to gather berries and greenery for an Advent wreath, assembled while we listen to Christmas music and share treats and a pot of tea. Even at very young ages, my children have delighted in this creation of something beautiful and meaningful from the ordinary materials of our neighborhood. Each Sunday of Advent, we tuck a few more candles into the wreath and have a candlelight dinner, singing carols and reading passages of Scripture aloud. Sometimes Sunday turns into Tuesday before we can make it happen, and with small children at the table these evenings can feel more squirmy than sacred, but they still serve to reorient our hearts. They help anchor our celebration of Christmas in the story of the Kingdom, creating space within all the seasonal merriment for our lament and longing and our defiant hope as we wait for our returning King.

> They help anchor our celebration of Christmas in the story of the Kingdom.

My children have not yet experienced much of this longing or this hope, and thus the depths of what we celebrate at Christmas are only beginning to unfold for them. For now, they revel in Christmastime as a season of good cheer, happy memories, presents, treats, family time, and delightful traditions. These things are good, and these things matter: they are strong threads weaving us together, and when hard times come upon a family, as they inevitably do, I have seen how they help keep the fabric from unraveling. And yet I hope that our celebration of

Christmas gives my children more than happy days and warm memories to draw upon for strength and comfort, and certainly more than the secular liturgies of nostalgia, sugar, plastic, and generic good will. I hope our Christmases are a means of inviting them to participate ever more deeply in all that is most real and true, of rooting them in a sense of place and belonging and kinship and story. I pray that these can truly be holy days as well as merry ones, turning their faces toward the Light that shines in darkness and will never be overcome.

Week 4:
Remembering the Future

Remembering the Future

This week begins with the glorious "Hallelujah" chorus (don't forget to stand while it plays) and ends on Day 25 with "Worthy is the Lamb." We have a future and a hope! Truly this is a week for rejoicing and enjoying, too. Need I tell you, tired mama, not to get so caught up in the trappings that you forget to enjoy? The singing, candles, Bible readings, and food will be remembered long after the toys have broken.

I am famous for stressing out over trying to make sure I get the exact number of gifts for each of my children or at least spend the same amount of money. One year in late spring, I picked up a journal in the drawer by my reading chair and found an entry someone else had written:

> "I feel like giving it all up. I cannot really go on with my life. I didn't get as many presents as my other siblings which makes me think my parents don't love me."

At first I took this at face value, all my fears of leaving someone out racing in to horrify me, until I realized my silly son Christopher had been home over the holidays and left me a note to laugh about!

Advent Hymn

Hark! the Herald Angels Sing

CHARLES WESLEY

Hark! the herald angels sing,
"Glory to the newborn King:
peace on earth, and mercy mild,
God and sinners reconciled!"
Joyful, all ye nations, rise,
join the triumph of the skies;
with th'angelic hosts proclaim,
"Christ is born in Bethlehem!"
Hark! the herald angels sing,
"Glory to the newborn King"

Christ, by highest heav'n adored,
Christ, the everlasting Lord!
Late in time behold him come,
offspring of the Virgin's womb.
Veiled in flesh the Godhead see;
hail th'incarnate Deity,
pleased as man with men to dwell,
Jesus, our Emmanuel.
Hark! the herald angels sing,
"Glory to the newborn King"

Hail, the heav'n-born Prince of Peace!
Hail the Sun of Righteousness!
Light and life to all he brings,
ris'n with healing in his wings.
Mild, he lays his glory by,
born that man no more may die,

born to raise the sons of earth,
born to give them second birth.
Hark! the herald angels sing,
"Glory to the newborn King"
"Glory to the newborn King"

If you haven't sung "Good Christian Men Rejoice," "Good King Wenceslas," or any other of your favorite family carols, sing a few extra songs during Morning Time this week.

Advent Scripture Memory

Revelation 5:12-13

12 Saying with a loud voice, Worthy is the Lamb that was slain to receive power, and riches, and wisdom, and strength, and honour, and glory, and blessing.

13 And every creature which is in heaven, and on the earth, and under the earth, and such as are in the sea, and all that are in them, heard I saying, Blessing, and honour, and glory, and power, be unto him that sitteth upon the throne, and unto the Lamb for ever and ever.

Advent Poetry

A Christmas Carol

G K CHESTERTON

The Christ-child lay on Mary's lap,
His hair was like a light.
(O weary, weary were the world,
But here is all aright.)

93

The Christ-child lay on Mary's breast,
His hair was like a star.
(O stern and cunning are the kings,
But here the true hearts are.)

The Christ-child lay on Mary's heart,
His hair was like a fire.
(O weary, weary is the world,
But here the world's desire.)

The Christ-child stood at Mary's knee,
His hair was like a crown.
And all the flowers looked up at Him,
And all the stars looked down.

Advent Feast

Christmas Eve

The anticipation has reached its peak. Here we are on the very eve of Christmas. My favorite part of the week of Christmas is Christmas Eve. In our family, we have traditionally had a Christmas Eve party with various hors d'oeuvres, Christmas cookies, and sometimes singing. We end the evening by lighting candles and singing "Silent Night" together. It is my single favorite moment of the year.

Now that most of the children are adults, and not home for Christmas, we take our smaller family to our church's Lessons and Carols service on Christmas Eve. Here we also end the service with singing "Silent Night" with candles. Lessons and Carols are a very British way to celebrate the holiday. The first Festival of Nine Lessons and Carols was held at King's College in Cambridge in 1918. In this annual traditions, nine readings from the Bible are each followed by two Christmas carols or hymns. This service has inspired churches all over the world to hold their own Lessons and Carols servies. If you don't have a service near you, you can often find Lessons and Carols services broadcast online during the season.

In early December the University of the South in Sewannee, Tennessee has a traditional Lessons and Carols service in their gorgeous cathedral-like chapel. If you ever get a chance to attend, don't miss it. You will be transported. You could even create your own Lessons and Carols by gathering Bible readings and carols, singing after each Bible reading. A sample "homemade" Lessons and Carols is on page 118.

On our Christmas Eve, after we eat, open our Angel gifts, and sing, any little people go to bed. Tim and I finish wrapping presents, set out unwrapped presents, and set the table for a glorious Christmas morning breakfast, usually dropping into bed late and a bit hyped up from a preview of the chocolate.

Besides "Silent Night," Christmas Eve is a good time to sing "O, Holy Night." It is truly one of the most magnificent carols of the season. My all-time favorite version of this song is sung by Twila Paris and Matthew Ward. Now is the time to fall on your knees. Advent is almost over—Christmas is here!

Listening to Handel's *Messiah*

Greg Wilbur

The first day of listening in Week 4 closes out the Part 2 section of *Messiah* with the very familiar "Hallelujah" chorus. In this choral work the praise of the angels and the elders and the great clouds of witnesses call back and forth around the throne of God as a fitting reminder that death cannot hold Christ—for he is the King of kings and Lord of lords forever and ever.

Part 3 begins with the soprano Air "I Know That My Redeemer Liveth" and establishes this section with a settled, peaceful and sure declaration of faith in the risen Lord. In the chorus, "Since by Man Came Death," the music moves back and forth through representations of the first Adam who brought sin into the world by the Fall and the second Adam (Christ) who breaks the powers of sin. The specter of death is conveyed through the slower sections with melodic tension and chromatic harmonies; the hope of resurrection is sung to comparatively open major harmony with an energetic tempo.

Appropriately, the bass Air "The Trumpet Shall Sound" includes a prominent use of trumpet as soloist and as a counter-melody to the vocal soloist. The setting of the word "changed" seems to move the soloist from one place to another in an upward movement.

The entire work ends with a stately and full declaration of "Worthy the Lamb That Was Slain." Notice the difference in the music setting when the choir sings about the Lamb who was slain and when the choir sings about what the Lamb will receive (powers, riches, wisdom, and strength). The main section of this movement concludes with a statement of the text "forever and ever" that evokes the end of Part 2 and the "Hallelujah" chorus. Following this is a multi-layered "Amen" that covers nearly ninety measures and brings the entire work to a majestic close.

Although all three sections depict Christ, *Messiah* is infrequently performed in its totality. More typical performances include the "Christmas" sections in December and the "Easter" sections in the spring. Usually all performances include the "Hallelujah" chorus. While it is easy to see why choir directors would make those choices for the sake of time and practice, the flow of Scripture from the need for a Savior, the coming of the Messiah, the death and resurrection of Christ, and the conquering of death and His position of authority at the right hand of the Father are portrayed throughout the fullness of the work. Listening to the entirety of *Messiah* allows for the richness of the person and work of Christ to fill this holiday season with the glory of the Gospel, the promise of redemption, and the anticipation of both the first and second comings of Christ.

Cindy's Listening Schedule

Day 19
(6 minutes)

Scripture Reading

Psalm 2:4

4 He that sitteth in the heavens shall laugh: the Lord shall have them in derision.

Psalm 2:9

9 Thou shalt break them with a rod of iron; thou shalt dash them in pieces like a potter's vessel.

Revelation 19:6

6 And I heard as it were the voice of a great multitude, and as the voice of many waters, and as the voice of mighty thunderings, saying, Alleluia: for the Lord God omnipotent reigneth.

Revelation 11:15

15 And the seventh angel sounded; and there were great voices in heaven, saying, The kingdoms of this world are become the kingdoms of our Lord, and of his Christ; and he shall reign for ever and ever.

Revelation 19:16

16 And he hath on his vesture and on his thigh a name written, King Of Kings, And Lord Of Lords.

Listening

No. 42.   Recitative (Tenor) "He that dwelleth in heaven..."

> *He that dwelleth in Heav'n shall laugh them to scorn; The Lord shall have them in derision.*
> *(Psalm 2:4)*

No. 43. Air (Tenor) "Thou shalt break...."

Thou shalt break them with a rod of iron; thou shalt dash them in pieces like a potter's vessel.
(Psalm 2:9)

No. 44. Chorus "Hallelujah!!"

Hallelujah: for the Lord God Omnipotent reigneth.

The kingdom of this world is become the kingdom of our Lord, and of His Christ; and He shall reign for ever and ever.

King of Kings, and Lord of Lords.
Hallelujah
(Revelation 19:6, 11:15, 19:16)

Day 20
(5 ½ minutes)

Messiah Part 3

Scripture Reading

Job 19:25-26

25 For I know that my redeemer liveth, and that he shall stand at the latter day upon the earth:

26 And though after my skin worms destroy this body, yet in my flesh shall I see God:

I Corinthians 15:20

20 But now is Christ risen from the dead, and become the firstfruits of them that slept.

Listening

No. 45. Air (Soprano) "I know that my Redeemer..."

I know that my Redeemer liveth, and that He shall stand at the latter day upon the earth.
And though worms destroy this body, yet in my flesh shall I see God. (Job 19:25-26)

For now is Christ risen from the dead, the first fruits of them that sleep.
(I Corinthians 15:20)

Day 21
(2 minutes)

Scripture Reading

I Corinthians 15:21-22

21 For since by man came death, by man came also the resurrection of the dead.

22 For as in Adam all die, even so in Christ shall all be made alive.

Listening

No. 46.   Chorus "Since by man...'

Since by man came death, by man came also the resurrection of the dead.
For as in Adam all die, even so in Christ shall all be made alive.
(I Corinthians 15:21-22)

Day 22
(5 minutes)

Scripture Reading

I Corinthians 15:51-53

51 Behold, I shew you a mystery; We shall not all sleep, but we shall all be changed,

52 In a moment, in the twinkling of an eye, at the last trump: for the trumpet shall sound, and the dead shall be raised incorruptible, and we shall be changed.

53 For this corruptible must put on incorruption, and this mortal must put on immortality.

Listening

No. 47. Recitative (Bass) "Behold, I tell you a mystery..."

> *Behold, I tell you a mystery; we shall not all sleep, but we shall all be changed in a moment, in the twinkling of an eye, at the last trumpet.*
> *(I Corinthians 15:51-52)*

No. 48. Air (Bass) "The trumpet shall sound..."

> *The trumpet shall sound, and the dead shall be raised incorruptible, and we shall be changed.*
> *For this corruptible must put on incorruption and this mortal must put on immortality.*
> *The trumpet. . . da capo*
> *(I Corinthians 15:52-53)*

Day 23
(10 minutes)

Scripture Reading

I Corinthians 15:54-57

54 So when this corruptible shall have put on incorruption, and this mortal shall have put on immortality, then shall be brought to pass the saying that is written, Death is swallowed up in victory.

55 O death, where is thy sting? O grave, where is thy victory?

56 The sting of death is sin; and the strength of sin is the law.

57 But thanks be to God, which giveth us the victory through our Lord Jesus Christ.

Listening

No. 49. Recitative (Alto) "Then shall be brought..."

> *Then shall be brought to pass the saying that is written: "Death is swallowed up in victory."*
> *(I Corinthians 15:54)*

No. 50.   Duet (Alto, Tenor) "O Death, where..."

> *O death, where is thy sting? O grave, where is thy victory?*
> *The sting of death is sin, and the strength of sin is the law.*
> *(I Corinthians 15:55-56)*

No. 51.   Chorus "But thanks be to God..."

> *But thanks be to God, who giveth us the victory through our*
> *Lord Jesus Christ.*
> *(I Corinthians 15:57)*

Day 24
(5 minutes)

Scripture Reading

Romans 8:31-34

31 What shall we then say to these things? If God be for us, who can be against us?

32 He that spared not his own Son, but delivered him up for us all, how shall he not with him also freely give us all things?

33 Who shall lay any thing to the charge of God's elect? It is God that justifieth.

34 Who is he that condemneth? It is Christ that died, yea rather, that is risen again, who is even at the right hand of God, who also maketh intercession for us.

Listening

No. 52.   Air (Alto) "If God be for us..."

> *If God be for us, who can be against us?*
> *(Romans 8:31)*

> *Who shall lay anything to the charge of God's elect? It is God*
> *that justifieth, who is he that condemneth? It is Christ that died,*
> *yea rather, that is risen again, who is at the right hand of God,*
> *who makes intercession for us.*
> *(Romans 8:33-34)*

How Our Family Celebrates

Kelly Cumbee

Jesus said, "I am the light of the world;
whoever follows me will not walk in darkness,
but will have the light of life."[6]

The house is almost completely dark and we are all gathered in the living room. The children are walking around, bumping into each other and laughing. Before anyone has time to get hurt, my husband says, "The people walking in darkness—" he strikes a match and continues, "have seen a great light!"

"Thanks be to God!" we all say, and my husband reads more Scripture and prays while I light the first candle in the Advent wreath.

Lighten our darkness, we beseech thee, O Lord; and by thy great mercy defend us from all perils and dangers of this night; for the love of thy only Son, our Savior, Jesus Christ.

We have entered the Advent season this way for a quarter of a century now, and our traditions have grown as our family has.

---

6   John 8:12 (ESV)

Our first Advent wreath, which I made the second Christmas we were married, was just four votives arranged around a tray and surrounded by greenery I'd cut from the boxwoods in front of our apartment. We didn't really know what we were doing back then, and I don't remember us having any special prayers or Scripture readings for that first Advent lighting, but I do remember the music. We had a Christmas album collection which included several selections from *Messiah*. These were my favorites because the choir of the church I'd grown up in sang the well-known arias and choruses from it every December. In time I found a little book of Advent devotions which we used for years while lighting the candles. For the last dozen years we've used our church's Evening Prayers and Scriptures from the lectionary.

Almighty God, give us grace that we may cast away the works of darkness, and put upon us the armor of light, now in the time of this mortal life in which thy Son Jesus Christ came to visit us in great humility . . .

At the beginning of Advent, we set out the nativity scene: the stable, the shepherd, and all the animals. Mary and Joseph begin their journey at the northern end of the house, and my son who will always approach the holidays with the delight of a four-year-old moves them along each day so that they arrive just before we go to church on Christmas Eve. After coming home we add Baby Jesus and the angels, and hang a star above the stable. That night too, or the next day, the three Wise Men set out from the East, and arrive on Epiphany, January 6th. By this time, the shepherds and animals have "gone back to the fields"—meaning of course, that my son has moved them to another part of the room—and the stable has become a house.

O God, Make speed to save us.
O Lord, make haste to help us.

For years we didn't put up the Christmas tree till late in the

Advent season, which was how my family did it when I was growing up, but several years ago my childlike son started asking us to put it up right after Thanksgiving, so we compromised—we buy a tree as soon after Thanksgiving as we can manage, but it's an Advent Tree until Christmas Eve.

When we set it up, we put the star on top and add all the lights, but we only light them on Sundays in Advent. We make ornaments called Chrismons™,[7] each with a symbol for Christ—a fish, a cross, a crown of thorns—and place those on the tree, talking about what they mean. Every Sunday during Advent, we turn on the tree's lights just before Evening Prayers and add a few silver and purple ornaments so that the tree grows more festive as we get closer to Christmas Day. Then on Christmas Eve, we take off most of the Advent ornaments and add all the Christmas ones. At the church's Christmas Eve service it's now officially Christmas, so when we come home we turn on all the tree lights, including the star on top, and leave them on the whole season of Christmas and Epiphany.

> When we set it up, we put the star on top and add all the lights, but we only light them on Sundays in Advent.

O gracious Light,
pure brightness of the everliving Father in heaven,
O Jesus Christ, holy and blessed!

When the children were young they loved making paper snowflakes and hanging them from the light over the dining room table and sticking them to the big window in the school room. One daughter specializes in decorating the rooms with greenery and lights, which she starts putting up a couple of weeks into Advent—

---

7   "Chrismon" is a portmanteau combining "Christ" and "monogram." Chrismons™ are Christmas decorations made with Christian symbols. The idea for Chrismons originated with Ascension Lutheran Church in Danville, Virginia, in 1957 by Mrs. Frances Kipps Spencer, who trademarked the name.

we love the long, slow build-up to Christmas, the gradual brightening of our home as the days are becoming darker.

My soul doth magnify the Lord,
and my spirit hath rejoiced in God my Savior... [8]

And of course there's music! My oldest son serenades us with "Grandma Got Run Over by a Reindeer," and the Straight No Chaser version of "The Twelve Days of Christmas." Someone is usually practicing choir music, and we're singing the hymns of the season during our Evening Prayers. I play music for half an hour or so before Morning Prayers each day, and the selection is usually from whichever composer we're focusing on, but in Advent I start playing Handel's *Messiah*. I used to play only the Christmas parts of it, but many years ago Cindy inspired me to make sure we play the whole thing over the course of Advent. Then, starting on Christmas morning I play Bach's *Christmas Oratorio*, which is arranged for most of the Twelve Days of Christmas. My youngest son still says that listening to *Messiah* during Advent is his favorite tradition, and my children still sing "A pink-white sheep!" when it plays (you might think this chorus is really "All we like sheep," but my children are convinced that their way is correct). And we all love caroling. When all the children are home we have a full choir and love surprising our friends by showing up on their doorsteps singing in four-part harmony, "Angels We Have Heard on High," and other favorites. We even take requests!

Our father, who art in heaven,
hallowed by thy Name...

---

8   Luke 1:46-47

My favorite part of the season will always be the liturgy of Evening Prayers by the light of the Advent wreath, with all the Scripture readings, and the canticles and hymns we sing. A few years ago we learned that the verses of the hymn "O Come, O Come, Emmanuel," were traditionally sung as antiphons to the *Magnificat*, the heartfelt Song of Mary—"My soul proclaims the greatness of the Lord"—in the last few days before Christmas Eve, so we've added that tradition to our liturgy. Beginning on December 17th, each night we sing one verse before and after the *Magnificat*, starting with "O come, thou Wisdom from on high," and ending with "O come, O come, Emmanuel" on the 23rd. Mary praises God for remembering his promise of mercy, "The promise he made to our fathers, to Abraham and his children for ever," and our yearly remembrance of that promise kept builds our faith in him and all his promises. And so I close with our church's traditional Advent Blessing:

> *May Almighty God, by whose providence our Savior Christ came among us in great humility, sanctify us with the light of his blessing and set us free from all sin. Amen.*
>
> *May he whose second Coming in power and great glory we await, make us steadfast in faith, joyful in hope, and constant in love. Amen.*
>
> *May we, who rejoice in the first Advent of our Redeemer, at his second Advent be rewarded with unending life. Amen.*
>
> *And the blessing of God Almighty, the Father, the Son, and the Holy Spirit, be upon us and remain with us for ever. Amen.*[9]

Go in peace to love and serve the Lord.
Thanks be to God!

---

9   Quotes from collects and canticles in this essay are taken from The Book of Common Prayer (1979) of The Episcopal Church, Church Publishing Incorporated, New York.

Christmas Fulfilled

Merry Christmas!

And now the day we have been waiting for has arrived! Christ is born. Emmanuel, God with us! We can hardly contain the joy and excitement. When our children were small, they woke us up in the wee small hours in order to open presents. When they got older, the younger children woke the older children until all were grown up enough to contain their joy for a few extra hours of sleep.

As we all assemble around the Christmas tree, my husband Tim reads the Christmas story from Luke 2, and then one by one we open our presents. When all 11 of us were together this could take hours. Sometimes we were so bogged down we let several people open presents at once. In years of plenty we had to stop midway to eat our beautiful breakfast at our beautiful table. Now, we can generally eat breakfast after the gifts. And soon there will be that Christmas morning when Tim and I wake up to find all the birds have flown. We can be thankful that while our family had sad times as well as happy times, our Advents were almost unequivocally joyful, from Thanksgiving to Christmas.

We always gave each of the children a book for Christmas, concentrating on nice hardbound copies, but some years we were happy just to give any book. When we could, we used these gifts to add to our library collection. For a few years, we were collecting Asterix comics. When we lived near the Brandywine River Valley Museum in Chadd's Ford, Pennsylvania, and had the opportunity to see the N. C. Wyeth collection there, we focused on collecting the lovely Scribner Illustrated Classics which Wyeth illustrated.

My parents always rounded out our gifts with all the noisy, battery-operated toys they could afford, and the children loved them for it. We also had stockings hanging up somewhere. We usually saved them for after breakfast. Just when it seemed like everything was over, someone remembered the stockings!!

Our breakfast always included egg casserole, cinnamon rolls, fruit, and eventually, mimosas. By the time breakfast was over, Tim and I were ready for our naps and the kids were ready to read and play.

In 2001, as we noticed how everyone felt "blah" after the festivities, we thought it might be fun to go to the movies on Christmas Day. A new tradition was born that year when we went to see *The Fellowship of the Ring*. It turned out to be a great way to end the day. So now I put the rib roast in the oven, and when it is time to turn it off and let it sit in the oven, we head to the movies. When we return home, we all dig into rolls, roast beef, and horseradish sauce. Christmas is a two-meal day with generous amounts of chocolate filling in the gaps. Our favorite recipes for Crown Roast Beef with Horseradish Sauce and Rollins Rolls are on pages 132-133.

For our family, the holidays are coming to a close. We will straggle through the week after Christmas celebrating one birthday and the new year, but the major festival of the year is now over. I enjoy a couple weeks of recovery by reading, reading, and reading. We are then all ready to return to normalcy, but not without the memory that we are a Christian family and we have a Messiah.

Day 25: Christmas!
(6 minutes)

Scripture Reading

Revelation 5:12-13

12 Saying with a loud voice, Worthy is the Lamb that was slain to receive power, and riches, and wisdom, and strength, and honour, and glory, and blessing.

13 And every creature which is in heaven, and on the earth, and under the earth, and such as are in the sea, and all that are in them, heard I saying, Blessing, and honour, and glory, and power, be unto him that sitteth upon the throne, and unto the Lamb for ever and ever.

Listening

No. 53.   Chorus "Worthy is the Lamb..."

*Worthy is the Lamb that was slain, and hath redeemed us to
God by His blood, to receive power, and riches, and wisdom,
and strength, and honour, and glory, and blessing.
Blessing and honour, glory and power, be unto Him that sitteth
upon the throne, and unto the Lamb, for ever and ever.
Amen.
(Revelation 5:12-14)*

Extras

The Advent Wreath and Candles

Each Sunday in Advent, an additional candle is lit in the Advent wreath. Here is the meaning traditionally understood by each candle.[10]

Week 1: Prophecy Candle

The first candle reminds us of the Old Testament prophecies of the coming Messiah, such as Genesis 3:15.

Week 2: Bethlehem Candle

The second candle is the Bethlehem Candle, reminding us of the way in which God prepared Israel for the coming Messiah. When this week's candle is lit, often Micah 5:2 is read.

Week 3: Shepherd's Candle

The third candle reminds us that the shepherds were the first to receive the glorious tidings of Christ's birth. Luke 2:8-18 gives the account of the shepherds (see page 51-52).

Week 4: Angel's Candle

The fourth candle reminds us of the angels and the part God gave them in preparing people for the coming of the Messiah and announcing His birth. When lighting this candle, passages such as Matthew 1:18-21, Luke 1:30-33 and Luke 2:8-14 are read.

Christmas Eve: The Christ Candle

The white candle is lit on Christmas Eve to show that the waiting is over! It is time to celebrate the birth of Christ!

Why is one candle pink?

The Shepherd's candle is traditionally pink to represent the joy of the shepherd's worship and our joy knowing Christmas is nearing. After the Shepherd's candle is lit, we are half-way through Advent!

---

10   There are many resources for learning more about Advent wreaths. Here is one: http://clearnotesongbook.com/liturgy/advent

Lessons and Carols

Each year the King's College Cambridge[11] presents The Festival of Nine Lessons and Carols service on Christmas Eve. Although every year's service is a little different, the service always begins with the hymn "Once in David's Royal City."

Taking a little inspiration from the Festival, here are some suggested Scripture readings and familiar carols you might like for your own Lessons and Carols.

First Lesson: Genesis 3:8-19
"O Come, O Come, Emmanuel"

Second Lesson: Genesis 22:15-18
"Angels from the Realms of Glory"

Third Lesson: Isaiah 9:2, 6-7
"Come, Thou Long-Expected Jesus"

Fourth Lesson: Isaiah 11:1-3a; 4a; 6-9
"Lo, How a Rose E'er Blooming"

Fifth Lesson: Luke 1:26-35, 38
"What Child is This?"

Sixth Lesson: Luke 2:1, 3-7
"Away in a Manger"

Seventh Lesson: Luke 2:8-16
"God Rest You Merry, Gentlemen"

Eighth Lesson: Matthew 2:1-12
"We Three Kings"

Ninth Lesson: John 1:1-14
"O Come, All Ye Faithful"

---

11   Learn more about King's College Cambridge and the Festival of Nine Lessons and Carols: https://www.kings.cam.ac.uk/chapel/a-festival-of-nine-lessons-and-carols

https://en.wikipedia.org/wiki/Nine_Lessons_and_Carols

Twenty Christmas Books

Picture Books:

1. *Papa Panov's Special Day* by Ruben Saillens, adapted by Leo Tolstoy, retold by Mig Holder, illustrated by Tony Morris
2. *Stephen's Feast* by Jean Richardson, illustrated by Alice Englander
3. *Jolly Old Santa Claus* by Alice Leedy Mason, illustrated by George Hinke. An Ideal publication. (*I love all the Ideals Christmas books.*)
4. *The Year of the Perfect Christmas Tree* by Gloria Huston, illustrated by Barbara Cooney
5. *The Church Mice at Christmas* by Graham Oakley
6. *The Christmas Day Kitten* by James Herriot
7. *Take Joy: Tasha Tudor's Christmas Book* by Tasha Tudor
8. *Christmas with Little Women* by Louisa May Alcott, illustrated by Russ Flint
9. *The Nutcracker* by ETA Hoffman, adapted by Janet Schulman, illustrated by Renee Graef. *Another favorite Nutcracker book is by Deborah Hautzig, illustrated by Diane Goode.*
10. *The Mitten* by Jan Brett (*And don't miss all the other Jan Brett books.*)

Other Books:

11. *A Christmas Carol* by Charles Dickens
12. *The Chimes* by Charles Dickens
13. *The Best Christmas Pageant Ever* by Barbara Robinson
14. *The Shepherd, the Angel, and Walter the Christmas Miracle Dog* by Dave Barry
15. *Shepherds Abiding* by Jan Karon
16. *The Birds' Christmas Carol* by Kate Douglas Wiggins
17. *The Christmas Stories of George MacDonald* illustrated by Linda Hill Griffith (*I like the 1981 edition by David C. Cook.*)
18. *The Lion in the Box* by Marguerite De Angeli
19. *Turkey for Christmas* by Marguerite De Angeli
20. *Christmas Spirit* by George Grant and Gregory Wilbur

Songs Mentioned in this Book

Featured Hymns

"O Come, O Come, Emmanuel" and "Veni, Veni, Emmanuel" (Week 1) - p. 24-26, 106-107, 118

"Come, Thou Long Expected Jesus" (Week 2) - p. 50, 118

"O, Come All Ye Faithful" and "Adestes Fideles" (Week 3) - p. 72, 118

"Hark! the Herald Angels Sing!" (Week 4) - p. 50, 92

Other Sacred Music

"Angels from the Realms of Glory" - p. 118

"Angels We Have Heard on High" - p. 105

"Away in a Manger" - p. 118

"God Rest You, Merry Gentlemen" - p 118

"Good Christian Men, Rejoice!" - p. 93

"Good King Wenceslas" - p. 93

"Listen my Son" written and performed by Judy Rogers, from the album *Go to the Ant* - p. 54

"Lo, How a Rose E'er Blooming" - p. 118

"O Holy Night" performed by Twila Paris and Matthew Ward, from the album *It's the Thought* - p. 95

"O, Little Town of Bethlehem" - p. 50

"O, Sing a Song of Bethlehem" - p 50

"Once in David's Royal City" - p. 50, 118

"Silent Night" - p. 94, 95

"We Three Kings" - p. 118

"What Child is This?" - p. 118

Other Christmas Favorites

"Grandma Got Run Over by a Reindeer" - p. 106

"He's Too Fat for the Chimney," by Irving Gordon, performed by Gisele Mackenzie from the album *Christmas by Gisele* (1957) - p. 13

"Jingle Bells"- p. 54

"Rockin' Round the Christmas Tree" - p. 54

"Rudolf the Red-Nosed Reindeer" - p. 54

"Silver Bells" - p. 55

"The Twelve Days of Christmas" - p. 106

"White Christmas/Whiter than Snow" performed by Twila Paris, from the album *It's the Thought* - p. 55

Advent Recipes

I have two favorite cookbooks which are based on the church calendar.

- *Bless This Food: Four Seasons of Menus, Recipes and Table Graces* by Julia M. Pitkin and Karen B. Grant and George Grant
- *A Continual Feast: A Cookbook to Celebrate the Joys of Family & Faith throughout the Christian Year* by Evelyn Birge Vitz

I also use old family recipes, *Southern Living* cookbooks, and Christmas cookbooks.

The Feast of St. Nicholas

St. Nicholas's feast day is traditionally celebrated with molded cookies. A couple years ago I bought a beautiful old-fashioned St. Nicholas mold. I found my own shortbread recipe worked pretty well in the mold, and you cannot beat a good old butter cookie for flavor, but you can also find recipes and ideas for cookie molds online.

Scotch Shortbread

1 cup butter. *I like salted butter.*

1 cup sugar. *Granulated sugar works better than honey for molded cookies.*

2 cups flour. *King Arthur or White Lily. We want our gluten to be glutenous, somewhat like our hips.*

1. Preheat oven to 300°.
2. Cream butter and sugar. This is the most important step. Mix in flour with hands if necessary.
3. Spread dough on oiled mold or in square baking pan. Cut in pan and perforate before baking to get that Walker look.
4. Bake for 30 to 40 minutes.
5. Let cool and remove from mold. Pick up all the broken pieces and eat them. You can dip these in chocolate or you can decorate your molded St. Nick.

The Feast of St. Lucia

Nobody, nobody can make bread and rolls like my mother. Even when I copy her recipe exactly, even when I watch her movements perfectly, my own rolls never turn out quite as delicious as hers. It makes the truth that she will not always be around profound. We will miss her. We will miss her rolls. Here is her recipe for Swedish Tea Ring. May the touch of my mother, Judy Ward, be with you.

Swedish Tea Ring

Sweet Roll Dough

We like Betty Crocker's recipe.

2 packages of active dry yeast

1/2 cup warm water. *Not so hot as to kill the yeast, but hot enough to activate it.*

1/2 cup warm milk. *Let it cool enough that it will not kill the yeast.*

3/4 cup sugar

1 tsp salt

2 eggs

1/2 cup shortening or butter, softened. *I like to do some of each.*

4 1/2-5 cups flour *like White Lily or King Arthur all-purpose flour* .

1. Dissolve yeast in warm water with a bit of the sugar and salt. Let it proof for 10 minutes. If it doesn't bubble up start over with new yeast.
2. Stir in milk, sugar, salt, eggs, shortening and 2 1/2 cups of flour. Beat until smooth. Mix in the some of the remaining flour until dough is smooth and easy to work. Less flour is better.
3. Knead dough in mixer for 5 minutes. Place dough in greased bowl and turn over to cover all areas with grease. Cover with a towel and let rise in warmish place until it doubles. About 1 1/2 hours.
4. Punch dough down. Shape into desired rolls.

This is the basic recipe for the rolls. We will shape them into a Swedish tea shape.

Shaping the Tea Ring:
1/2 of your Sweet Roll Dough (see above)
2 or more Tbsp butter
1/2 cup packed brown sugar
2 tsp cinnamon
1/2 cup raisins

To decorate after baking:
Powdered sugar icing
Pecans and candied cherries

1. Roll dough into a 15x9 inch rectangle. Spread the dough with butter. Sprinkle with sugar, cinnamon and raisins. Roll dough up, beginning with the longer side, pulling it toward you slightly as you roll. Seal the edges. Mush it around to make the shape even.
2. Lay this roll of dough in a circle on a greased baking sheet. Pinch the two ends together. Now you are going to make cuts 2/3 of the way through the dough in 1-inch sections. Lay each section on its side. Let this rise until doubled.
3. Bake at 400° for 20 minutes. Watch carefully. Underdone is better than overdone.
4. Drizzle icing made from powdered sugar and milk over the warm ring. Decorate with pecans and cherries for a festive look.

Christmas Cookies

Maxwell Family Crescents

1 stick butter

1 cup flour

1 cup finely chopped nuts. *I usually stick with finely chopped pecans.*

4 Tbsp powdered sugar

1. Work dough with hands and form into crescent sticks.
2. Bake at 350-400° about 12 minutes until done (pay attention).
3. Roll in powdered sugar while warm.

Chocolate Oatmeal Cookies

12 oz package of chocolate chips (semi-sweet preferred)

1/2 cup butter

3/4 cup sugar

2 eggs

1 tsp vanilla

2 cups rolled, old-fashioned oats

1 1/2 cups flour

2 tsp baking powder

1/4 tsp salt

1/2 cup powdered sugar

1. Heat oven to 350°.
2. Melt 1 cup of chocolate chips. *Tricky, tricky... Sometimes I melt more for extra chocolate flavor.*
3. Beat together butter and sugar until light and fluffy.
4. Blend in eggs, vanilla and melted chocolate.
5. Add combined dry ingredients, not including powdered sugar.
6. Stir in remaining chocolate chips.
7. Shape into 1-inch balls and roll in powered sugar, coating heavily.

8. Place on ungreased cookie sheet. Bake for 10 minutes. Do not overbake. Cook on wire rack.

Makes about 5 dozen.....well of course not, I think I made about 3 dozen out of this recipe yesterday.

Rollins Family Sugar Cookies and Icing
(Adapted from Betty Crocker's Ethel's Sugar Cookie)

3/4 cup shortening (part butter)
1 cup sugar
2 eggs
1 tsp vanilla
2 1/2 cups flour
1 tsp baking soda
1 tsp salt

1. Mix shortening, sugar, eggs, and flavoring thoroughly.
2. Stir flour, baking powder, and salt together; blend in.
3. Chill at least 1 hour.
4. Heat oven to 400°.
5. Roll dough 1/8-inch thick on a lightly floured board.
6. Cut with 3-inch cookie cutter. Place on an ungreased baking sheet.
7. Bake 6 to 8 minutes, or until cookies are a delicate golden color. While the cookies are cooling, I make Sugar Cookie Icing, which is on the next page.

Makes about 4 dozen. I make the cookies in lots of different shapes: bells, Santas, Christmas trees (the favorite shape), little hands, gingerbread people, etc.

Sugar Cookie Icing

powdered sugar

milk

vanilla (no vanilla in the white)

food coloring (various)

We cover our big dining room table with wax paper and set out the icing and sugars, etc. We make about 6 colors of icing with extra red, white and green. We paint the cookies with the icing and add all kinds of sugars and drops to decorate. We let the cookies dry.

Someone judges who decorated the best Santa and the best overall cookie. Then I try and save the cookies from immediate destruction, via eating, for our neighbors and friends and also our own Christmas Eve party. I also freeze some for New Year's Eve.

I make a lot of cookies.

Chocolate Macaroons

1 package Devil's Food Cake Mix

1 cup flaked coconut, toasted

1/2 cup rolled oats, toasted

3/4 cup butter, melted

2 tsp vanilla

2 eggs, slightly beaten

6 Hershey bars (or several chocolate chips per cookie)

3/4 cup shredded coconut

1. Combine first 6 ingredients.
2. Chill.
3. Drop dough by heaping teaspoons 2 inches apart on ungreased cookie sheets.
4. Bake at 350° for 10 minutes.
5. Immediately top each hot cookie with 1 chocolate square or a few chocolate chips.
6. Spread to frost.
7. Sprinkle with shredded coconut.

Our Traditional Christmas Eve

Cheese Straws

You can't really claim to be a southerner without cheese straws for the holidays.

2 cups grated sharp cheddar cheese
2 Tbsp sugar
1/4 tsp red pepper
2 cups all-purpose flour
2 sticks butter, softened
1/4 tsp salt

1. Preheat oven to 350°.
2. Mush this all together with your hands or in a food processor, but hands are better.
3. Shape into crescents, placing on ungreased baking sheet.
4. Bake for 10 minutes. Cool and eat.

Cracker Candy

2 sleeves butter flavored crackers like Ritz Crackers, broken into
    big pieces.
3/4 cup butter
3/4 cup firmly packed brown sugar
2 cups milk chocolate morsels. *Or any flavor, really.*
Chopped pecans

1. Preheat oven to 350°.
2. Line a 9x13-inch pan with greased aluminum foil.
3. Spread with crackers.
4. Bring butter and brown sugar to a boil in a medium saucepan, stir continually. Cook for 3 minutes continuing to stir.
5. Pour mixture over crackers.
6. Bake for five minutes.

7. Turn oven off and sprinkle cracker mix with chocolate chips. Let stand in warm oven until the chocolate has melted. Spread the chocolate evenly over the cracker mix and sprinkle with pecans. Let cook and then break into pieces.

Crockpot Wassail

Lynn Bruce

Right before bedtime on Christmas Eve, I assemble this in a large slow cooker and set it on warm overnight. First thing Christmas morning, I turn it to high. Once it is piping hot, we like to remove the lid and enjoy the festive aroma wafting through the house.

1 lemon
1 orange
1 small red apple
1 gallon apple cider
1 jar pineapple juice (32 oz)
1 jar unsweetened cranberry juice (32 oz)
1-2 cups strong black tea (optional)
2-4 cinnamon sticks
1 Tbsp dried allspice berries
1 tsp whole cloves
Optional: a splash of orange juice

1. Set the slow cooker on a large cutting board or platter (to protect surface from sticky drips and hours of heat), well out of the reach of children.
2. Pour about half of each jar of juice into the crock, then add more of each to taste. Take care not to overfill the crock because liquids expand slightly when heated.
3. Thinly slice the orange and lemon. Stud the apple with cloves.
4. Put allspice berries in a stainless steel tea ball, or tie up in a small square of cheesecloth.
5. Add all to the crock, and toss in the cinnamon sticks. Allow to

simmer a while to release spices.

6. Serve hot in mugs.

Reserve the remaining juices to top off crock as needed throughout the day's festivities.

Cindy's Christmas Day Breakfast

Egg Casserole

All amounts are guesses. I have long since lost this recipe and I make it by feel. Prepare egg casserole on Christmas Eve, refrigerating until baking Christmas morning.

4 cups cubed bread. *Play with different kinds. Hawaiian rolls are excellent.*

1 lb. roll of mild or hot sausage. *Crumbled and cooked through.*

4 cups shredded sharp cheese. *Again, try different cheeses.*

6 eggs. *Obviously, this is the basic recipe, I have been known to quadruple it.*

2 cups milk

1 tsp sugar

1 tsp red pepper

1. Place bread cubes, cooled sausage, and cheese in a large bowl or kettle.
2. In another bowl or with stand mixer, beat eggs and milk together.
3. Add sugar and pepper to egg mixture and pour over bread mixture in the large bowl.
4. Grease a large baking pan and pour mixture into the pan.
5. Place in the refrigerator overnight.
6. Bake at 400° until center is cooked through. Time depends on the pan.

Our Favorite Cinnamon Rolls

Makes 20 very large rolls.

1/2 cup warm water (105°-110°)
2 scant Tbsp active dry yeast
2 tsp granulated sugar
1 (3 1/2 oz) pkg instant vanilla pudding (*the key*)
Cold milk to make the pudding according to package directions
1/2 cup butter, melted
2 eggs, beaten
1 tsp salt
8 cups bread flour (*all-purpose will also work*)
1 cup butter, melted
Frosting of choice. *I just use powdered sugar, milk, and vanilla.*

1. In a small bowl, combine water, yeast, and sugar; stir until dissolved. Set aside.
2. In a large bowl, make pudding mix according to package directions. Add butter, eggs, and salt; mix well. Add the yeast mixture; blend. Gradually add flour and knead until smooth, adding "sprinkles" of flour as needed to control stickiness. Once the dough is no longer sticky and is soft and silky feeling (like a baby's bottom), the dough is ready.
3. Place in a very large buttered bowl and flip dough over so the buttered side is up. Cover and let rise until double in bulk (about 1 hour).
4. Punch down, flip over so buttered side is up, and let rise again (about 45 minutes).
5. On a lightly floured surface, roll out to a 34"x 21" rectangle.
6. Spread 1 cup of melted butter over surface.

Filling

2 cups brown sugar, firmly packed

4 tsp cinnamon

1. In a small bowl, mix sugar and cinnamon. Sprinkle all over the surface of the rolled-out rectangle of dough, leaving an inch on one long side (this will be the outside edge of your "jelly roll"). Roll up very tightly. The trick is to pull the dough toward you as you roll it away from you. Use a coffee mug or a couple of unopened cans of food to keep what you've rolled from unrolling while you work on the other end of the roll.

2. With a knife, put a notch every 2 inches along the top of the roll. Cut a 12-18" length of unflavored, waxed dental floss. Place floss under the roll along each notch and criss-cross the ends over the top, pulling them around the roll against one another to make a nice clean cut.

3. Place rolls on greased or buttered baking pan, 2" apart. Lightly press rolls down with your hands, just a little, to help them hold together.

4. Cover and let rise until double.

5. Bake at 325° for 18-20 minutes. Take them out when they JUST start to turn golden. DON'T OVERBAKE THEM! Frost warm rolls.

Christmas Day Dinner at the Rollinses'
My favorite Christmas evening meal.

Crown Roast Beef with Horseradish Sauce

1 7-10 lbs. standing rib roast
Salt
Pepper

1. The night before cooking, leave open in the refrigerator in order to allow a crust to form.
2. Take it out 3-4 hours before cooking, letting it warm to room temperature.
3. Preheat oven to 500°. Cover the roast with salt and pepper. I like to use chunky salt and pepper.
4. Multiply the pounds of your roast by 5. So a 6-pound roast would need to cook for 30 minutes.
5. Set the roast in a pan, fat side up.
6. After the roast has cooked the exact number of minutes you calculated, turn the oven off *without checking on the roast or opening the oven door*. Do not open the oven door. This is when we leave for the movies at our house. Leave the roast in the oven for 2 hours....*see, you can go to a movie!* If using a meat thermometer, you want to see it reach 130°.
7. Take the roast out. Let it sit for 5 minutes, then slice and dip in horseradish sauce.

Horseradish Sauce

Adapted from Bless This Food *by Julia M. Pitkin with George and Karen Grant.*

1/4 bottle horseradish, drained and dried
1 Tbsp vinegar
1/2 tsp dry English mustard

1/2 tsp salt

1/2 tsp pepper

1/2 cup heavy cream

1. Mix all the ingredients together, except the heavy cream, in a small bowl.
2. Beat the cream until stiff.
3. Fold the mixed ingredients into the whipped cream.
4. Dip the roast beef into the horseradish sauce.

Serve with Rollins Rolls or Yorkshire Pudding.

Rollins Rolls (**Our family's dinner rolls**)

1 package of active dry yeast

1/4 cup warm water (*not so hot as to kill yeast but warm enough to activate it.*)

3/4 cup of scalded, then cooled, lukewarm milk

1 egg

3/4 cup sugar

2 1/4 tsp salt

1/4 cup butter

4 1/2 cups all-purpose flour. *Any combination of white and whole wheat works.*

1. Proof the yeast by dissolving it in the warm water with a pinch of salt and sugar. If it is bubbling up within 5 minutes, it is good to go. If not, get better yeast.
2. Mix together proofed yeast, milk, sugar, salt, egg, and butter. Mix in 2 1/2 cups of flour. Gradually begin adding in remaining flour to form a soft dough. Less flour is better. Knead dough with mixer or by hand for 5 minutes until smooth and elastic.
3. Place in greased bowl and turn to coat. Let rise for about 2 hours.
4. Punch dough down and divide into rolls. Place on a greased pan so that when they rise they will touch each other. Cover

and let rise about an 1 hour.

5. Bake at 400° for 10-12 minutes. They taste better when they are not overbaked.

6. Brush with butter while warm.

Epiphany Recipes

Not-So-Traditional King Cake
Kerry Williamson

As a young mom, I often had expectations for festal celebrations that exceeded my available time and abilities. Perfection was the enemy of the good too often! While this cake is certainly not traditional, it allowed us to make Mardi Gras a fun part of our family history. Incredibly easy and quick!

This cake can be served anytime from Epiphany to Mardi Gras (the Tuesday before Ash Wednesday – the beginning of Lent).

2 cans store-bought cinnamon rolls (*Look for roll, rather than biscuit-type cinnamon rolls. Pillsbury Cinnamon Rolls work really well*)
Sugar sprinkles: yellow, green, purple
A dried bean or small plastic toy baby to serve as your "baby Jesus"

1. Preheat oven to 375° (or the temperature recommended on the cinnamon roll packaging).

2. Remove cinnamon rolls from package and flatten slightly to make an oval rather than circular shaped roll. Lay rolls in a flattened ring, overlapping edges of the rolls. You want the resulting shape to look somewhat like a flower.

3. Bake according to package directions. Let cool.

4. Frost with the icing included with the rolls. Sprinkle on yellow, green, and purple sprinkles. (*This looks best if done in sections of one color each.*) Serve, or store for up to 24 hours. Definitely best when eaten the first day.

If you include the "baby Jesus," warn your guests! And consider having a small gift ready for the winner or a crown. Traditionally, the one who finds the "Jesus" hosts the next Mardi Gras celebration.

Traditional French Galette des Rois
(Cake of the Kings or Kings' Cake)
Kerry Williamson

While this seems very fancy, it is quite easy to make, if you purchase puff pastry. You should be able to find frozen puff pastry in most grocery stores. Of course, you can make your own, if you are so inclined. This galette is a STUNNER on a plate! Serve with tea or coffee...and pass out paper crowns for a festive Epiphany celebration. If you chose to include the "baby Jesus" (a dried bean), you might like to have a small gift ready for the one who finds it!

For the Frangipane (Almond Cream Filling)
½ cup almond meal
¼ cup granulated sugar
1 egg
3 Tbsp butter, softened
¾ tsp vanilla extract
1 Tbsp all-purpose flour

For the Galette
1 batch frangipane (above)
17 oz puff pastry, thawed
1 egg, beaten
1 dried lima bean "baby Jesus" (optional)
2 Tbsp confectioners' sugar

1. Combine the ingredients for the frangipane in the bowl of a food processor. Blend to a smooth, creamy paste. You've made frangipane! The frangipane can be made a few days in advance (keep refrigerated in an airtight container).

2. Preheat the oven to 425° F.

3. Roll out the sheets of puff pastry and cut out two 11-inch circles. Place the first circle on a parchment-lined baking sheet, then cover it in in an even layer of frangipane. Leave about a 1-inch border around the edge of the circle.

4. If you plan to use the dried bean (*traditional, but not at all necessary*), now is the time to press it lightly into the frangipane. Lightly dampen the 1-in border around the first pastry circle (*this will help seal the two pastry pieces together*). Place the second puff pastry circle on top of the first. Crimp the edges with a fork to seal.

5. Brush the galette with the beaten egg and bake for 15 minutes at 425°. Dust the cake with powdered sugar and bake for an additional 10 minutes or so, until the pastry becomes a deep golden color. There may be spots of dark brown—this is ok! Allow the galette to cool for 20 minutes.

Serve with tea or coffee. If you include the dried bean "baby Jesus," make sure to warn your guests!

Contributors

Thomas Banks

Thomas Banks has taught great books with an emphasis on Greek and Roman literature, Latin grammar and ancient history for more than ten years both as a private tutor and as a junior high and high school teacher in his native Idaho and Montana. He holds a dual bachelor's degree in English Literature and Classical Studies from the University of Idaho, from which he graduated in 2008. In the summer of 2019, he moved to North Carolina to marry the illustrious Ms. Angelina Stanford, who said yes for some reason.

Poetry is a particular love of his, and he has published original verse and translations in *First Things*, the St. Austin Review and various other periodicals. His personal list of favorite writers never really stops growing, but will always include Homer, Euripides, Virgil, Ovid, St. Augustine, Shakespeare, Samuel Johnson, Byron, Keats, Walter Scott and Thomas Hardy. Of these and so many others one cannot have enough.

Thomas Banks currently resides in North Carolina, where he teaches Latin, literature and history online with his wife Angelina Stanford at *The House of Humane Letters*. His poetry, translations and other writings have appeared in *First Things*, *The Imaginative Conservative*, *The New English Review*, and various other publications.

Greg Wilbur, M.M.

Gregory Wilbur is Dean of the Chapel, Dean of the College, permanent Trustee and Senior Fellow at New College Franklin. Mr. Wilbur received a B.A. in Music with a minor in English followed by a M.M. in Composition, both from the University of Alabama.

In addition to his role at New College Franklin, Mr. Wilbur is the Chief Musician of Cornerstone Presbyterian Church (PCA) and is the author of three books, numerous articles and speaks regularly on the arts, worship, and education. Mr. Wilbur has composed award-winning works for choir, orchestra and corporate worship as well as commissions. He lives in Franklin with his wife Sophia, daughter Eleanor, and dog Sparky.

Kerry Williamson

Kerry Williamson and her husband Erik live in North Carolina where they have raised their family of four since 1996. The Williamsons have been homeschooling since 2003 and hope to continue until their youngest's graduation in 2027. Kerry has been involved with a classical education co-op since 2006, where she currently leads the senior class. She also teaches high school literature to homeschoolers in the local community. Erik is the Executive Director of Missionary Support Services, which provides "back office" services for missionaries all over the world. Kerry and Erik have enjoyed traveling—often with children—to many different parts of the world including: Europe, Asia, Africa and many parts of the United States.

Lynn Bruce

Lynn Bruce is an Ambleside Online Founding Advisory member. She grew up on a wheat and cattle farm in north central Texas, the daughter of a minister. Her mother, having been a voice major in college, passed along to Lynn early on her love for classical music and traditional hymns sung in acapella harmony, and taught her solfa as a child. Throughout her school years, Lynn's interests included studying classical piano, art, and competing in UIL (University Interscholastic League) Poetry Interpretation and Drama contests. Through these interests she developed a lifelong relationship with great music, art, poetry and literature. She feels all of these early exposures continue to define and enrich her life, and she is grateful to have the opportunity through AmblesideOnline to help make great literature and the fine arts accessible to her own children and many others. Lynn graduated magna cum laude from Texas Tech University with a BS in Education, emphasis in Generic Special Ed (a junior year switch from Fine Arts), and taught briefly in public school.

Lynn's daughter, Caitlin, who spent her school years as one of the first Advisory guinea pigs for AmblesideOnline and House of Education, is happily married and recently earned her master's degree in Creative Writing, summa cum laude, from UTD. Lynn's daughter Claire is currently a senior at UTD, studying to be a professional dance therapist. Her son Justin is a college student.

Caitlin Bruce Beauchamp

Caitlin Bruce Beauchamp is a homeschooling mother, writer, and pastor's wife. She lives in Texas with her husband and three small children. Caitlin is a graduate of AmblesideOnline and earned a B.A. and M.A. in the Humanities with an emphasis in creative writing from the University of Texas at Dallas.

Kelly Cumbee

Kelly Cumbee is the mother of seven children whom she has educated at home from the beginning. For the first 18 years of their marriage, her husband, Mike, was enlisted in the military, so she managed this not only through many pregnancies, but through many moves and on a minimal budget. Her four daughters and three sons range in age from 17 to 31, and include a special needs son who will always live at home. Her homeschooling style is an organic outgrowth of her love for nature, story, music, and tradition.

Special Thanks to New College Franklin

Wisdom
Discipleship
Service

The Great Tradition
and the Classical Seven Liberal Arts
with a Biblical Foundation.
A four-year conversation
that prepares you for
Life

physical address: 136 3rd Avenue South, Franklin, TN 37064
mailing address: PO Box 1575, Franklin, TN 37065
615-815-8360 | newcollegefranklin.org

About the Author

Cindy Rollins

Cindy Rollins homeschooled her nine children for over thirty years. She is a co-host with Angelina Stanford and Thomas Banks of the popular *Literary Life Podcast* and curates the "Over the Back Fence Newsletter" at CindyRollins.net. She is the author of *Mere Motherhood: Morning Time, Nursery Rhymes, and My Journey Toward Sanctification*; *A Handbook for Morning Time*; and the *Mere Motherhood Newsletters*.

Cindy runs an active Patreon group where the participants read Charlotte Mason's volumes and discuss questions pertaining to motherhood and life. Her heart's desire is to encourage moms using Charlotte Mason's timeless principles. She lives in Chattanooga, Tennessee, with her husband, Tim, and dog, Max. She also travels around the country visiting her 13 grandchildren, watching her youngest son play baseball, and occasionally speaking at events.

You can find her at her website **CindyRollins.net** where she publishes her newsletter "Over the Back Fence."
Facebook https://www.facebook.com/cindyrollins.net/
Instagram https://www.instagram.com/cindyordoamoris/
Twitter https://twitter.com/CindyOrdoAmoris
Mere Motherhood Facebook Community Group https://www.facebook.com/groups/meremotherhood/

Books By Cindy Rollins

Mere Motherhood: Morning Time, Nursery Rhymes, and My Journey Toward Sanctification
Mere Motherhood Newsletters
Handbook to Morning Time
Hallelujah: Cultivating Advent Traditions with Handel's Messiah

Other Blue Sky Daisies Titles

Geography Books
Elementary Geography by Charlotte Mason
Home Geography for Primary Grades with Written and Oral Exercises by C. C. Long

Language Arts and Grammar Books
The Mother Tongue: Adapted for Modern Students by George Lyman Kittredge. In this series: Workbook 1 and 2; Answer Key 1 and 2
Exercises in Dictation by F. Peel
Grammar Land: Grammar in Fun for the Children of Schoolroom Shire (Annotated) By M. L. Nesbitt. Annotated by Amy M. Edwards and Christina J. Mugglin

The CopyWorkBook Series
The CopyWorkBook: George Washington's Rules of Civility & Decent Behavior in Company and Conversation by Amy M. Edwards and Christina J. Mugglin
The CopyWorkBook: Comedies of William Shakespeare by Amy M. Edwards and Christina J. Mugglin

Other Titles
The Birds' Christmas Carol by Kate Douglas Wiggin
The Innkeeper's Daughter by Michelle Lallement
Kipling's Rikki-Tikki-Tavi: A Children's Play by Amy M. Edwards

*These titles are popular with those inspired by Charlotte Mason and her educational philosophy.

Made in the USA
Las Vegas, NV
04 October 2023